C0-AVH-889

FREE PLAY

FREE PLAY

Organization and Management
in the
Pre-school and Kindergarten

By

EILEEN GRACE COWE, Ed.D.

Department of Curriculum and Teaching
Hunter College, City University of New York
New York, New York

CHARLES C THOMAS • PUBLISHER
Springfield • Illinois • U.S.A.

136878

Published and Distributed Throughout the World by
CHARLES C THOMAS • PUBLISHER
2600 South First Street
Springfield, Illinois 62717, U.S.A.

This book is protected by copyright. No part of it
may be reproduced in any manner without written
permission from the publisher.

© *1982 by* CHARLES C THOMAS • PUBLISHER
ISBN 0-398-04647-6
Library of Congress Catalog Card Number: 81-21346

*With THOMAS BOOKS careful attention is given to all details of
manufacturing and design. It is the Publisher's desire to present books that are
satisfactory as to their physical qualities and artistic possibilities and
appropriate for their particular use. THOMAS BOOKS will be true to those
laws of quality that assure a good name and good will.*

Printed in the United States of America

I-RX-1

Library of Congress Cataloging in Publication Data

Cowe, Eileen Grace.
  Free play.

  Bibliography: p.
  Includes index.
  1. Play.   2. Kindergarten--Methods and manuals.
I. Title.
LB1140.35.P55C68   372.13   81-21346
ISBN 0-398-04647-6   AACR2

PREFACE

THIS book deals specifically with the Free Play or Choice Period in a pre-kindergarten or kindergarten class. Some teachers interpret the Free Play Period as a play time when children do as they want and go from one activity to another with little or no supervision from adults. This period is the heart of the program for young children. It needs to be organized and managed so that it promotes language and intellectual development that helps to secure a firm foundation for the formal instruction of reading, writing, and spelling soon to follow. It provides children with opportunities to select materials and equipment so that they can explore, test, examine, create, discover, experiment, and observe for a given amount of time. It also gives opportunities to talk about their endeavors and experiences.

Little or no real instruction about organizing and managing a Free Play Period has been given to teachers. The purpose of this book is to give specific detailed instructions to teachers, student teachers, or any adult working with young children for setting up, conducting, and managing Free Play or Choice Period, beginning with the first day of school.

Another feature is a chapter on each center of interest or activity that comprises the Free Play Period. The necessary equipment for the centers, where it can be purchased, and how to arrange and introduce it are given. The learning implications inherent in each activity or center of interest are discussed, as well as techniques for improving the quality of play within the center.

A chapter giving instruction on how to incorporate the subject matter areas of art, math, science, social studies, and language arts into the Free Play Period is unique.

This book has evolved from my experience with preschool and kindergarten children from different socioeconomic levels, student teachers, and college classes in early childhood education.

Every child has the need for (and therefore the right to) a learning environment in which he or she has many opportunities to think clearly and speak spontaneously in both individual and group situations. A well-run program for a Free Play or Choice Period does this and at the same time paves the way for future academic pursuits.

CONTENTS

136878

138878

FREE PLAY

Chapter 1

HISTORY

PRIME among the regular experiences every preschool and kindergarten child should have are those various activities classified as free play. These provide the learning environment in which children have many opportunities to think clearly and speak spontaneously in both individual and group situations. A well-run program of free play arouses the child's curiosity and interest and stimulates his or her creativity. It helps the child grow intellectually, emotionally, and socially. In many ways, regular involvement in these activities paves the way for future academic pursuits.

The operational goal of the free play or choice period is a pre-kindergarten or kindergarten classroom of twenty-five young children busily engaged in five to ten different activities while the noise level remains minimal.

Such a happy situation comes about only by careful planning, organization, and management. The desirable style of functioning in the classroom is one in which groups of children are working simultaneously and quietly in various areas of the room. For example, three or four children are in the block area; four or five are in the housekeeping area; two are painting; two or three children are using the woodworking bench; three or four are using puzzles, Tinkertoy® construction toys, touching boxes, or other materials at the table; one or two are using mathematical equipment; and some are looking at books.

Too often, teachers have been admonished to provide these experiences but have been given little or no real instruction as to how to achieve the operational situation just described. The single

3

exception is one chapter in *Curriculum Is What Happens,** published by the National Association for the Education of Young
Children (NAEYC). This authors intends to give many specific,
detailed instructions to the teacher for setting up, conducting,
and managing the free play or choice period in early childhood
classrooms.

The importance of this part of the preschool kindergarten program may be more readily understood by reviewing the evolve-
ment of early childhood education.

In the first part of the nineteenth century, the idea of children
learning through play was conceived by Friedrich Froebel, a
German who had great respect for the young child and his ability
to learn. Froebel opened his kindergarten, translated a "child's
garden," in the little village of Blankenburg, Germany, in 1837.

Froebel had spent the previous fifteen years designing and
developing a total program of "gifts and occupations." The "gifts"
were a set of permanent play materials designed to give the child
familiarity with the geometric forms and their derivation and to
lead him to a better understanding of himself and his world.
"Occupations" was a term given to a type of handiwork that included clay modeling, the interlacing of paper strips, and building
forms with sticks connected by softened peas. The occupations
were to extend and fix the impressions made by the gifts.

Not only did Froebel devise the gifts and occupations but he
described with great precision and detail the manner in which
children were to use them. Each gift and occupation was to be
used alone until all possible meanings were pursued; then, they
were to be utilized in combinations with other gifts for expansion
and extension of ideas. It might require weeks for the children and
teacher to complete the manipulation of each one and the study
of all its meanings.†

Froebel suggested that play with the gifts could become a
group procedure, even though the more simple ones were suitable
for a mother with her child. Accordingly, he organized the first

---

*Dittman, Laura (Ed.). *Curriculum is what happens.* Washington, D.C.: NAEYC, 1970,
pp. 39-50.

†Personal communication by the author in January, 1975, with Edna O'Dea, who had
the Froebelian training at Hunter College, New York City.

group session, which he termed "kindergarten."

Because Froebel himself actively taught children, trained teachers, and supervised the instruction, as well as devising the materials and procedures, the Froebelian kindergartens were transported in toto to various locations.

The Froebelian kindergarten was taken first to England and later to America by two sisters who took Froebel's course in Hamburg, Germany, in 1848. Bertha and Margarethe Meyer were daughters of a wealthy manufacturer of liberal views. Bertha Meyer Ronge started the first kindergarten in London. In 1852, Margarethe visited her sister, met and married Carl Schurz, and emigrated to the United States.

In 1856, after moving to Watertown, Wisconsin, Margarethe Schurz started her Froebelian kindergarten for her two daughters and their four cousins. This was the first kindergarten in America, and it was conducted in German.

A chance meeting of Elizabeth Peabody and Margarethe Meyer Schurz led to the opening of an English-speaking kindergarten in 1860 on Pickney Street in Boston. Eager to learn more about Froebel's kindergarten, Elizabeth Peabody made a trip to Europe in 1867. When she returned home, she traveled about the East Coast of the United States speaking in behalf of kindergarten education and encouraging people to start kindergartens.

In 1869, Milton Bradley was in the audience of one such meeting in Springfield, Massachusetts, and was an immediate convert. The kindergarten movement now had a disciple who would manufacture the necessary gifts and occupations.

Elizabeth Peabody's enthusiasm was instrumental in Maria Boelte's coming from Germany to start a Froebelian kindergarten in the Gramercy Park area of New York City. Later, she married Dr. John Kraus, and together they established the New York Seminary for training kindergarten teachers. In 1877, they published *The Kindergarten Guide** — the bible for young women taking the Froebelian training. In 1873, Miss Susan Blow, who had studied at New York Seminary, incorporated a Froebelian kinder-

---

*Kraus-Boelte, Marie & Kraus, John. *The kindergarten guide first volume.* New York: E. Steiger & Company, 1877, 453 pp.

The kindergarten guide second volume. New York: E. Steiger & Company, 1882, 418 pp.

garten into the public schools of St. Louis, Missouri.

The first modification of the Froebelian kindergarten was made by Anna E. Bryan in Louisville, Kentucky, in 1887. She questioned the rigidity of the Froebelian methods and began to introduce her own innovations in her teacher training school, known as the Louisville Free Kindergarten Association.

Into this environment of experimentation came Patty Smith Hill, a teacher who permitted the children to play imaginatively with the gifts, making paper dolls to fit the beds that were constructed out of the third and fourth gifts. The kindergarten in Louisville, Kentucky, attracted many visitors, and soon Froebel's materials and methods were being questioned by other educators.

In 1905, James Earl Russell, Dean of Teachers College, Columbia University, invited Patty Smith Hill to lecture at Teachers College. Susan Blow, the acknowledged leader of the Froebelian group, was already giving lectures there. From 1905 to 1909 these two educators gave courses together. Miss Hill, the younger of the two, championed her philosophy and ideas, and Froebel's materials and methods were gradually put aside. She insisted on a curriculum relevant to children's lives. It was she who created large blocks, child-sized housekeeping equipment, large pegboards, puzzles, and other materials. The emphasis was on providing the children with independent creative activities before embarking on the three Rs. This was known as free play, activity period, or choice time.

While Patty Smith Hill and her coworkers were reforming the kindergarten curriculum in the United States, Maria Montessori, a physician in a psychiatric clinic, worked out a series of sense-training exercises and a set of equipment for use in the training of mental defectives in Rome, Italy. Later, these materials were used with the education of young normal children.

In 1913-14, Madame Montessori lectured in America, and Montessori schools were opened. Soon, William Heard Kilpatrick, professor at Teachers College, made a trip to Italy and wrote a critical appraisal of the Montessori method, pointing out the limitations of the system as he saw it. Interest in the Montessori method declined rapidly and did not return until the late 1950s.

In 1923, Patty Smith Hill and the teachers in the Horace Mann School at Teachers College published *A Conduct Curriculum for the Kindergarten and First Grade.* * This monograph translated theory into practice and was based on years of research and innovation. It gave the teacher a wealth of activities and materials and their learning potentials. However, it failed to give teachers any real assistance in organizing a free play or activity period.

Caroline Pratt contributed the unit blocks to kindergarten education. She studied with Patty Smith Hill and in 1913 opened the Play School at Hartley House in New York City. She made all of her own equipment. Her innovative school attracted the attention of Lucy Sprague Mitchell, who went on to establish the well-known present-day Bank Street School and College.

Burke, Agnes et al. *A conduct curriculum for the kindergarten and first grade.* New York: Charles Scribner's Sons, 1923.

Chapter 2

EARLY CHILDHOOD MOVEMENT

FROEBEL'S prediction that his kindergarten would find full expression in America was a reality by the late 1920s. However, Froebelian methods and materials were no longer being used. They had been replaced by Patty Smith Hill blocks, Caroline Pratt's unit blocks, child-sized housekeeping equipment, dolls, a book corner, large puzzles, pegboards and pegs, and water and sand play. Teachers did not dictate a precise way to use them as they had done with the Froebel gifts and occupations. Children were encouraged to use them in free and creative ways.

For a period of time, the major innovations were maintained. Eventually, however, as the idea, methods, or techniques were passed along, the reform began to lose some of its original thrust.

Many kindergarten teachers failed to see the learning implications of the various activities and materials within the reformed kindergarten curriculum. Functioning in an era that fostered permissiveness in child rearing, the term of free choice of play activities advocated by Patty Smith Hill came to be interpreted simply as free play. To some teachers, free play meant an absence of giving directions, allowing children complete freedom to play at whatever they wished in almost any way, sometimes wandering from one play activity to another.

This manner of conducting the play period often led to noise and confusion. The lack of teacher planning with the child gave no sense of purposeful pursuit. The habit of aimless behavior in his free play period was poor preparation for the personal application needed for learning to read and to think and act responsibly.

World War II, the atomic bomb, and other scientific and technological developments awakened thinking Americans to the fact that life in America had no place for illiterates. Educators generally began rethinking the curriculum. Philip Phenix's article on *Key concepts and the crisis in learning** evoked considerable interest in 1956. His thesis was that each discipline has certain key concepts that could be used in teaching subject matter.

The following year (October 4, 1957), the Russians launched Sputnik. Almost immediately the educational system of United States was under attack. The kindergarten was not excluded from this criticism. It had not been questioned since Anna Bryan and Patty Smith Hill began their crusade to change Froebel's methods and materials back in Louisville, Kentucky, in 1887.

Following the Woods Hole conference in September 1959, Jerome S. Bruner† said that any subject can be taught to any child at any age in some honest form and suggested the spiral curriculum. A study conducted in five schools in the New York metropolitan area revealed that young children were capable of far more intellectual achievement than most parents or teachers believed possible.‡

Piaget's experiments with concrete examples and demonstrations of children's behavior gave scientific evidence of children's perceptions at various stages. In June 1964 at the University of Chicago, the Research Conference on Education and Cultural Deprivation reported that the best years of a child's learning are those years before the age of six.§

On January 12, 1965, President Lyndon B. Johnson announced the decision to fund Head Start, the antipoverty preschool program. The Head Start staff of the U.S. Office of Education embarked upon a long-range research project, coordinated by Stanford University, to determine the most effective way to

---

*Phenix, Philip. Key concepts, The crisis in learning. *Teachers College Record, 58*(3), 143, 1956.

†Bruner, Jerome S. *The process of education.* Cambridge, Massachusetts: Harvard University Press, 1960.

‡Wann, Kenneth D., Dorn, Miriam, & Liddle, Elizabeth Ann. *Fostering intellectual development in young children.* New York: Teachers College Press. 1962.

§Bloom, Benjamin S., Davis, Allison, & Hess, Robert. *Compensatory education for cultural deprivation.* New York: Holt, Rinehart & Winston, 1956.

teach low-income children. Known as Planned Variation, the pilot program had eight methods of teaching disadvantaged young children and followed them through the third grade. The models were located at University of Arizona; Ypsilanti Public School System; Berkeley, California; Newton, Massachusetts; University of Kansas; University of Illinois; University of Florida; and Bank Street College.

Additional research was carried on through the National Laboratory for Early Childhood Education, with its network of seven university-based centers at University of Arizona, University of Chicago, Cornell University, University of Kansas, George Peabody College, Syracuse University, and University of Oregon.

During this time, interest in the preschool child was at an all-time high. Many states and cities opened their first public school kindergartens. There was an urgency to help children develop further and faster in their academic pursuits. The common conception of learning by many people is that it begins with books and, therefore, with reading. To some, the obvious answer was to start reading instruction earlier. Unfortunately, in many cases, this simply meant moving down into the kindergarten those formal activities previously employed in first grade. Thus, in such classrooms, the instruction offered little or no opportunity for a child to select an activity and to consolidate his understanding through play and exploration.

Cohen and Rudolph* remind us that the assumption that only reading can offer information and provoke thought is a fallacy that underestimates the capacity for factual learning, generalization, problem solving, and cause-and-effect thinking of the preschool child. The reading of books is not a major source of learning for young children. Before learning to read, the child must have experience in firsthand, or sensorimotor learning. Piaget, the renowned psychologist, has said that early mental growth depends upon the child's opportunities for sensorimotor interaction. Children do not learn merely by watching or looking. They must have varied encounters with concrete materials. There is an old

---

*Cohen, Dorothy H. & Rudolph, Marguerita. *Kindergarten and early schooling.* Englewood Cliffs, New Jersey: Prentice-Hall, Inc., 1977, p. 14.

Chinese proverb that says "When I hear, I forget. When ↘
remember. When I do, I learn." The free play or choice ↕
provides opportunities to use materials and equipment so that
children can explore, test, examine, create, discover, experiment,
and observe. It also provides for opportunities to talk about endeavors and experiences. Stone* has rated the free play or choice
time as the heart of an early childhood program.

Elizabeth Jones says an effective teacher is one who (1) provides the child with choices, (2) enables him to consolidate his understanding through "messing about," through exploration of
materials and ideas at his own rate and in his own style, and (3)
interacts with him as resource and reenforcer to extend and vali-
date his choices and discoveries.† In subsequent chapters, this
author gives her techniques and ideas for setting up and main-
taining the free play or choice period in a pre-kindergarten or kindergarten classroom.

*Film, *Organizing Free Play*. B/W, 22 min. MTP 9053 Modern Talking Picture Service,
Inc., or Head Start, 1200 19th Street, N.W. Washington, D.C., 20505.
†Jones, Elizabeth. Introduction: curriculum planning in early childhood education.
Curriculum is what happens. In Dittman, Laura (Ed.), Washington, D.C.: NAEYC, 1970,
pp. 4, 5.

Chapter 3

ORGANIZATION OF
THE FREE PLAY OR CHOICE PERIOD

THE great end of....instruction is not to stamp our minds on the young, but to stir up their own, not to make them see with our eyes, but to work inquiringly and steadily with their own; not to give them a definite amount of knowledge but to inspire a fervent love of truth; not to form an outward regularity, but to touch inward springs; not to burden the memory, but to quicken and strengthen the power of thought...*

— William Ellery Channing

The Free Play or Choice Period is an ideal vehicle for implementing the philosophy of Dr. Channing, the noted Unitarian minister and contemporary of Elizabeth Peabody.

The Free Play or Choice Period should offer a variety of activities to accommodate the stages of developmental play: (1) solitary play, in which the child plays alone; (2) parallel play, in which the child plays alongside another child and usually enjoys being with him but is primarily interested in his own activity; and (3) cooperative play, in which the child is interested in other children. At age five, most children can engage in cooperative play with two to five children.†

---

*H. H. Cheetham. *Unitarianism and Universalism.* Boston: Beacon Press, 1962, p. 70.
†Hammond, Sara Lou, Dales, Ruth, Skipper, Dora, & Witherspoon, Ralph. *Good schools for young children.* New York: The Macmillan Company, 1963, pp. 244-245.

At the beginning of the school year, most children en~~j~~ solitary play or parallel play. Very little cooperative play ~~es~~ place except in the housekeeping and block areas. Even here, children revert back and forth from parallel to cooperative play. More cooperative play emerges as children mature and become acquainted with the materials.

Regardless of the maturity of the children, the teacher should always keep in mind that even though a child has reached the cooperative play stage, he needs opportunities for individual endeavors.

Materials should be highly manipulative and concrete rather than symbolic and abstract. The activities should be provocative, encouraging children to explore, investigate, and manipulate. Free Play or Choice Period should offer many choices to meet individual differences and promote self-direction in learning.

Often teachers are afraid of losing control of the children if a variety of activities are going on in the room at the same time. This is an unfounded fear. A well-planned environment with many choices automatically controls the behavior of a group of children. Then the teacher is freed for a substantial period of time, to observe children at work and play.* However, the kind of an environment that gives this free but controlled situation requires careful planning and organization.

The forerunner of a successful Free Play or Choice Period is arrival time. Every morning, the teacher should be at the door to greet the children, show them where to hang their coats, and give them assistance as needed. Careful attention to these details of starting the day will create a quiet, happy, relaxed climate that, ideally, can be monitored and maintained throughout the day.

During this arrival period the children should be permitted to converse with each other. They should not, however, speak in loud voices, shout, or run about the room. If the teacher converses in a quiet, well-modulated voice, the children will tend to copy her model.

---

*Jones, Dahle, and Pieters. Implementing a free choice program in public school kindergarten. In Dittman, Laura (Ed.), *Curriculum is what happens.* Washington, D.C.: NAEYC, 1970, p. 50.

Being at the door during arrival time gives the teacher an ideal opportunity to observe the children. Michael may have been in a fight on the way to school. Tony's sister, Sheryl, insists on bringing him inside the room, despite Tony's protests. Terry's appearance tells the teacher that he got himself ready for school. Steven says he did not have breakfast. Monica's mother is tearful about leaving her at school. Observing these incidents helps the teacher understand her children and respond in such a way as to alleviate problems that might arise to disrupt the climate of the classroom.

It is customary in most schools for all of the children to arrive at approximately the same time. When this is the case, as soon as they have removed their wraps, the children can be directed to the whole group assembly area. Or if preferred, each child may take a chair at a table. Then, when all are seated, the teacher can call two or three children at a time to come to the assembly area.

If the children arrive over a fifteen to thirty minute time span, they may be instructed to find a quiet activity, one for which the materials used can be put away quickly. Appropriate for this use are simple puzzles, Tinkertoys, books, beads, and small table toys.

As soon as all of the children have arrived, the teacher should assemble them in a semicircle in the area regularly used for total group activities. If the children have been engaged in an activity, the transition is made by the teacher designating two or three children at a time to put away their materials or equipment and to walk quietly to the assembly area. This transition should take only a few minutes and be done quietly with dispatch.

Initially, the teacher will have to assist the children in forming the semicircle. A chalk line or masking tape to indicate the assembly space will help the children find and keep their places. Each child should have a place where he can see and hear comfortably, with some space for shifting. Many educators frown upon the old-fashioned semicircle, but it provides an arrangement giving maximum viewing and hearing for the children.

An equally good arrangement for whole group activities is a fan shape, with the teacher at the apex. A corner of the room lends itself well to the fan arrangement. Regardless of the formation used, the teacher will need to assist the children in placing themselves so that everyone can see and hear well and not be too crowded.

The first activity of the school day is sharing. As soon as the children are seated, the teacher should take attendance. Then three or four children may be invited to share an experience with the group. The teacher may suggest such topics as a pet, a trip, a favorite toy or food.

For the first two weeks, encourage children to talk about something or to bring an object from home to share. However, as children become more accomplished in their speaking and use more time in making their reports, only a few children can be heard each day. The sharing period should be brief; too long a period leads to restlessness and inattentiveness.

A technique to make sure that each child has equal opportunity within a few days is to use three small containers or boxes. In the first container, place the names of all the children, each one on a separate slip of paper. Each day when the sharing period is held, three or four names can be drawn from the box to designate the children who will plan something to share with the class next day. As each name is drawn from the box, it should be placed in a second container. When the child has made his report, his name is moved into the third container. This procedure is continued until the first container is empty, indicating that all children have had a turn. Then all of the names are placed back in the first container and the rotation is repeated. Such a procedure locates the responsibility and distributes the opportunity for sharing. It is a simple organization that replaces the need for keeping a record of children who have participated.

For the first days, after sharing time, move the children back to the tables by designating small groups of two or three children to move at one time. As soon as they are seated at the table, give each one manila drawing paper and crayons. Direct them to use the crayons to make a pretty picture. Do not tell them what to draw; just encourage the children to use the materials. While the children are drawing, the teacher should put each child's name on his picture, so they can be easily distributed at dismissal. The making of the picture should not take too long, however, some children will spend more time than others. As soon as each child is finished, give him a table activity such as a simple puzzle, Tinker-toys, pegs, beads, etc. Confine the choice of activities to those that can be done while sitting at the table.

Allow the children about ten or fifteen minutes to engage in these table activities. During this time and also while they are making the picture, the teacher should talk to the children about what they are doing. If the children want to converse with each other, allow it but insist on quiet voices and confine the conversation to within each table. Do not permit talking or shouting back and forth between children at different tables.

When this period is over, the teacher calls two or three children at a time to put away the materials or equipment that they have been using. During transitions, the teacher compliments the children who are manifesting the kind of behavior she wants. This transition should be brief but unhurried.

For the first six or seven days, continue with this schedule of picture drawing followed by an activity. For the first two days, confine the activities to those that can be done while sitting. Have pegs, beads, books, Tinkertoys, etc., in sufficient quantities so that each child can have his own. Probably by the third day the children will be sufficiently accustomed to school that an activity away from the tables can be introduced.

Blocks are perhaps the best activity to add first. Designate three or four children to go to the block area. The behavior of the first children using the blocks will do much to set standards of block play for the year. Because of this, choose the first children carefully. To make your choice, think of children who would enjoy using blocks. These will be some of the more active ones. Among these, think of the ones who handle their bodies and materials with ease. You do not want a child who feels upset and might be inclined to demolish a structure as soon as it is built. Nor do you want an extremely boisterous child who would create excessive noise, or one who has such poor coordination that he would have difficulty in stacking the blocks. You do want children who handle the blocks easily and show evidence of enjoying cooperative play.

Also, by the third day of school, children will be able to choose among the table activities that they have been using. As each child finishes his picture, ask him which of the activities he would like to do. After each child makes his choice, he continues with that activity through the period. At this very early stage in his schooling, an important lesson for a child to learn is to commit himself to a task and carry it to completion.

On about the fourth day, introduce the housekeeping area; on the fifth day introduce the library area; on the sixth day, easel painting; and on the seventh day, water or sand play. By this time, all the basic activities except woodworking will have been introduced. Woodworking requires close supervision; so it is prudent to introduce it after the teacher is better acquainted with needs and interests of the children and after they can handle the other routines. This may be within a few weeks or not for two or three months.

In using this procedure there is a gradual introduction of activities, and the range of choices is gradually increased from a variety of table activities to blocks, housekeeping, easel painting, library, and so forth. At the same time, children are being guided and helped in making choices. They are also gradually becoming acquainted with the materials and equipment in the room. If everything is made available at one time, it very often is overwhelming to young children. They often flit from one activity to another or gravitate to pieces of equipment that are the most visible, so that within two or three days, ideas, habits, and patterns are set that do not contribute to their well-being or academic endeavors.

On the sixth or seventh day, eliminate the picture drawing activity. Immediately after roll call and sharing, initiate the choosing of activities by naming those available — table activities, blocks, housekeeping, library, painting, water play, and sand play.

Another way of helping children know the activities that are available is to use a bulletin board (Fig. 1). This idea can be introduced six or seven days after school has started. Mount pictures or realia to indicate each activity. For example, a picture of children using blocks, or a box containing a few small blocks attached to the bulletin board conveys the idea of the block area. In each case, the object or the picture may be labeled.

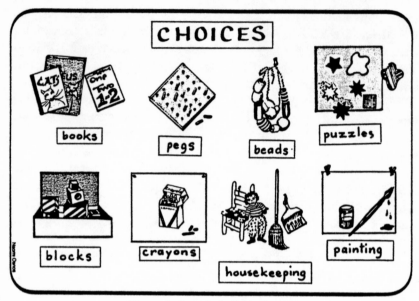

Figure 1. Sample bulletin board.

Often, children forget activities for the materials and equipment that are stored out of sight. The bulletin board serves as a visual reminder.

Each day as the children are choosing an activity they can look at the bulletin board and select what they want to do. If a child has decided to go to the block area but the block area is already filled with the four children it can accommodate, the child then selects something else from the bulletin board. Many children will be cognizant of the available activities and be able to choose quickly, while others will continue to need help. This bulletin board can remain up for several weeks, and new activities added as they are introduced.

During the choosing of activities, the teacher asks each individual child what he wants to do. At no time does she say, "all those wanting to build with the blocks go to the block area," or "the children wanting to paint go to the easels." Instead, she lets each child make his individual choice. The teacher must keep mental notes of the number of children that can be accommodated in the various activities, and when this number of children have chosen a specific activity, delete that one from the possible choices.

From now on each day after roll call and sharing, the teacher helps every child to select an activity. By taking time each day to give assistance in selecting an activity, the teacher is really saying by her actions, "You are expected to choose an activity and work with it. Your choice is important. I am interested in what you are doing."

As the teacher takes time to give this guidance, she has the opportunity to study and evaluate the children with whom she is working. If three or four children have repeated difficulty in selecting an activity, this might be a cue to let them be the first to choose. If a child insists on doing the same thing every day, it may be that he is comfortable doing this and is afraid of trying new things. In such cases, the teacher suggests and encourages in order to get him to try a new activity.

The teacher continues to use this procedure for choosing activities throughout the year. As the children become more accustomed to the routine, they will make their choices more easily and quickly. However, at no time does the teacher turn the class loose to go into the activities without each individual child making his own choice.

Elizabeth Jones* has stressed that in no case does the teacher take a laissez-faire role. Instead, she constantly assumes responsibility for assessing children's growth and learning. Accordingly, she must decide when a child needs a push, a boost, or a focusing or broadening of the stimuli in his learning environment. Her consistent goal is the promotion of self-direction in learning. To reach toward it, the teacher works to build self-confidence and competence in making choices and focusing attention on them. The learning environment that facilitates such growth is one that offers as many choices as the children within it can cope with and is flexible enough to meet the varying needs of different individuals at different times.

---

*Jones, Elizabeth. Introduction: curriculum planning in early childhood education. *Curriculum is what happens.* In Dittman, Laura (Ed.), Washington, D.C.: NAEYC, 1970, p. 5.

About two weeks after the opening of school, activities in the curriculum areas may be introduced. These are those relating to art, science, math, social studies, and language arts and organized to teach key concepts. Curriculum-related activities will involve additional pieces of equipment and materials to accommodate from three to six children daily. They are available for a limited time, perhaps five or six days, depending upon the total number of children in the classroom. The details of organizing and implementing these activities are discussed in the chapter on short-term activities (see Chapter 11).

Each day the teacher makes frequent visits to the various activities while children are involved. These visits will give her cues about adding additional materials. Her close observations will assist her in reevaluating the arrangement of equipment or materials for maximum efficiency. The perfect room arrangement in September might not be appropriate in December. The teacher should be very analytical about materials, equipment, and their placement in order to offer the children the best possible learning situation.

For example, if the teacher notices confusion among the children in the block area, it may be that the space is too small to accommodate all the children and their block structures. Either enlarge the space or reduce the number of children permitted in the area at any one time. A more orderly arrangement for storing and taking out the blocks may facilitate their use. If a child reaches over another child's structure to get a particular type of block he needs, this stretching and reaching may cause commotion. Rather than blaming the child or assuming that the activity is inappropriate for this particular class, the teacher should reevaluate the physical arrangement of the materials. Subsequent chapters give details about equipment and management of the various centers or activities.

The teacher's role during the Free Play or Choice Period is twofold once the children have selected an activity. First, she moves about giving encouragement, support, and guidance to the children, and second, she constantly analyzes and evaluates activities and the use of equipment and space in order to offer the best possible learning environment to these particular children.

The length of the activity period should be increased as the school year progresses and the children become able to participate in more complex activities. In the early part of the year, the Free Play or Choice Period may need to be quite short, perhaps twenty minutes. Once all of the activities are introduced, it should be increased to forty to fifty minutes. The teacher will become sensitive to signals indicating that the period should end. Such signals are loss of interest, leaving the activity, high and loud voices, and general pandemonium.

The teacher should keep a record of the children doing various activities. One way of keeping records is to type the names of the children on a master sheet and duplicate several copies. Then, when introducing a new activity, write the name of the activity at the top of a copy and check off the names of the children each day as they participate. By continuing this record keeping for all activities, the teacher has a record of the children who have done them.

In the space opposite each child's name can be noted details of the child's performance. This recorded information is valuable when conferring with parents and when planning for the child's growth. The notations will be helpful in examining each activity and the learnings that evolve from it.

At the end of the Free Play or Choice Period the children should be given an opportunity to report and to talk about the activities they have been involved in. Reporting should be introduced about the tenth or eleventh day of school and then conducted daily. All of the children participate, and only a few minutes is devoted to reporting time.

A chord on the piano, or three tones on the xylophone, or some other signal is given to get the children's attention, have them stop whatever they are doing, and find a place to sit down near the activity they have been pursuing. The teacher asks each child to tell what he has done during the activity period. For some children it will be an explanation of a construction built from blocks. The children in the housekeeping area may tell about the party they had, or they may only tell the roles they played, such as "I was the father" or "I was the mother." Another child may hold up the picture that he has painted. A child may report, "I worked with the puzzles."

In the first few days of reporting, some children may not be able to verbalize what they have done, and some children may not understand what they are to do. Then, the teacher should ask questions. In the case of some children, just holding up or showing their work or even pointing to something that they have worked with is certainly the beginnings of reporting. The teacher encourages each child to participate, even though he just points or says two or three words, and at no time should any highly verbal child monopolize these few minutes with lengthy descriptions of what he has done. The secret of a successful reporting session is to go quickly from child to child, confining the entire session to about ten minutes or less.

During this period only the child reporting is talking; the others are the audience and must be listening, and the teacher should insist on it. It is only courtesy to listen to each other. However, it may be necessary for the teacher to explain this to the children. A good supportive audience is just as important as a good speaker to a successful reporting session. The teacher should keep in mind that most young children do not know the behavior that is expected of them in a listening situation. Thus, the teacher needs to tell them and keep reminding and insisting that only one child talks at a time, while she and the others listen with interest.

The teacher shows genuine interest in each child and in his endeavors. By doing this she is saying to the child, "This is important — you have something worthwhile to share with us." The teacher should be cognizant of the fact that with guidance and experience, attention spans do increase, along with good listening habits and respect for fellow classmates. However, very rarely would a teacher spend more than ten minutes on reporting.

Many young children have never had the opportunity to express themselves verbally to a receptive audience. Reporting time gives the child this opportunity. If the child and his utterances are respected and dignified by the audience's giving attention, he will regard himself and his language more highly and will tend to improve. In sessions like this, each child has an opportunity to speak to an accepting audience, and the reporting lends dignity to both the child's utterances and his particular project or piece of work.

As the teacher works with the children, she will ask questions and encourage the children to ask questions of each other, thus generating thinking and encouraging intellectual development.

Strickland supports the premise that oral language fluency provides the basis for learning to read and write by saying that "the written form of language is learned after the child has gained proficiency in the use of the oral form."* Church; Herrick and Jacobs; Fries; Robison and Spodek; Cowe; and Wann, Liddle, and Dorn,† all concur that the child needs fluency in oral language before he is introduced to formal reading activities.

Teachers who conduct reporting sessions of work from the Free Play or Choice Period have found that discussions taking place over a period of time help the children learn to describe, clarify, and elaborate. Cowe‡ reported that something concrete to talk about was a factor that influenced the complexity and the amount of speech.

As teachers conduct daily reporting sessions, they are able to evaluate and study the children. The teacher observes those who can follow directions, recall an experience, be imaginative, be creative, and exhibit other skills that indicate progress emotionally, socially, and intellectually. In contrast to paper and pencil

---

*Strickland, Ruth. *The language arts in the elementary school.* Boston: D.C. Heath & Co., 1951, p. 97.

†Church, Joseph. *Language and the discovery of reality.* New York: Random House, 1963.

Herrick, Virgil E. & Jacobs, Leland B. *Children and the language arts.* Englewood Cliffs, New Jersey: Prentice-Hall, Inc., 1955.

Fries, Charles C. *Linguistics and reading.* New York: Holt, Rinehart and Winston, Inc., 1963.

Robison, Helen F. & Spodek, Bernard. In Wann, Kenneth D. (Ed.), *New directions in kindergarten.* New York: Teachers College Press, 1965.

Cowe, Eileen Grace. *A study of kindergarten activities for language development.* Unpublished doctoral dissertation, Teachers College, Columbia University, 1967.

Wann, Kenneth D., Dorn, Miriam Selchen, & Liddle, Elizabeth Ann. *Fostering intellectual development in young children.* New York: Bureau of Publications, Teacher College, Columbia University, 1962.

‡Cowe, Eileen Grace. *A study of kindergarten activities for language development.* Unpublished doctoral dissertation, Teachers College, Columbia University, 1967, pp. 86-87.

tests used with older children, the reporting session is an appropriate way for the pre-kindergarten and kindergarten teacher to evaluate.

Chapter 4

TABLE ACTIVITIES

FROEBEL'S conception of purposeful learning was one in which the child spent much time sitting at a table and manipulating certain materials according to instructions given by an adult. Some of the manipulative materials developed during the reform movement of the kindergarten were adaptations of Froebel's gifts. No doubt Parquetry Design Blocks were patterned after the seventh gift. Small table blocks similar to the blocks in the fifth and sixth gifts appeared.

The *Conduct Curriculum** listed pegs, boards, beads, tiles, color cubes, and puzzles as essential equipment. Through the years, other materials, such as Tinkertoys and more types of puzzles, became available. The children used these materials at the table, and soon they were referred to as table toys. During the past three decades, games and manipulative materials were developed in the curriculum areas of science, mathematics, and language arts.

A child enjoys and learns much from the manipulation of materials that allows experimentation. In the initial stages of using manipulative materials, the child is primarily interested in handling them and in finding out what pieces go together. As he becomes familiar with them, he sorts and classifies them according to various properties and uses. Next, he follows designs and instructions. Then finally, he creates his own designs.

The use of pegs and pegboards, the stringing of beads, and putting puzzles together help to develop eye-hand coordination.

---

*Burke, Agnes et al. *A conduct curriculum for the kindergarten and first grade*. New York: Charles Scribner's Sons, 1923.

The use of science and math materials leads to experimentation, observation, discovery, analysis, and logical thinking. Most manipulative activities offer the child the opportunity to work by himself. Self-satisfaction comes from things that teach us something. Patty Smith Hill states that "Something of the intellectual patience of the scientist is his when the child realizes that persistent, intelligent determination is the cost of success."*

Table activities are uniquely appropriate for the individual involvement; however, some games engage two to six children in cooperative activities. Games may be used to foster interest, knowledge, and skills in mathematics, science, and language arts. For example, ABC Lotto® games will acquaint children with letter location on a page and strengthen the powers of observation. Another example is Numberland®,† a game with engaging pictures on a board plus twenty sturdy plastic numerals. In order to move around the board the children must recognize colors and numbers and match correct quantities with the numerals.

Table activities are of a sedentary nature and are usually relatively quiet. Conversations often take place but little noise is generated. These activities help offset the noise from woodworking, blocks, and housekeeping areas, thus helping to balance the noise level in the room.

A good Free Play or Choice Time must have a variety of table activities available each day. The equipment for this area consists of various sizes of beads (plastic and wooden), bead string, various sizes of pegs and pegboards, counting frames, picture dominoes, nest of rings, nest of boxes, and other objects that nest according to shape and size. There should be puzzles varying from the simple (4 to 7 pieces) to the more complex (8 to 18), spelling blocks, lotto games, story boards, alphabet games, and Stori-Views®,‡ individual viewers with three-dimensional pictures. Science and mathematical equipment should consist of scales, magnifying glasses, magnets, measuring containers, play money, and number bingo.

---

*Garrison, Charlotte. *Permanent play materials for young children.* New York: Charles Scribners' Sons, 1926, p. x.
†Childcraft Education Corp. 20 Kilmer Road, Edison, New Jersey 08817
‡Stori-Views Division of Visual Data Corporation, Chesterfield, Missouri 63017

A doll house with an opening at the top rather than at the side permits the child to manipulate the furniture and doll characters at will. It should be one that may be assembled without screws or bolts to make a completely rigid structure, and the child should be able to disassemble it readily for convenient storage. Miniature furniture and flexible dolls are needed for this doll house.

The following companies have a plethora of excellent equipment that may be used in this area:

Childcraft Education Corporation
20 Kilmer Road
Edison, New Jersey 08817

Community Playthings
Rifton, New York 12471

Constructive Playthings
2008 West 103rd Terrace
Leawood, Kansas 66206

Milton Bradley Company
Springfield, Massachusetts 01101

J. A. Preston Corporation
71 Fifth Avenue
New York, New York 10003

Selective Education Equipment (science equipment)
3 Bridge Street
Newton, Massachusetts 02195

R. H. Stone Products
13735 Puritan
Detroit, Michigan 48227

Catalogs may be obtained by writing to the companies.

The equipment for table activities should be stored in cabinets or on open shelves and relatively near the tables and floor space where they are used. The storage space must be such that the equipment is within easy reach of the children. If a room is not equipped with adequate storage space, it may be necessary to purchase something. All of the companies listed have storage equipment, and Childcraft in particular has some unusual and versatile pieces.

Each classroom should have a good supply of equipment; however, only a portion is made available to the children at any one time. In the beginning days of working with the children, such items as beads, pegs, pegboards, simple puzzles (4 to 7 pieces), nest of rings, magnifying glass, and any other items that a child may use by himself are made accessible to him. Only items that are easy to use and require little or no direction or assistance from an adult are introduced in the beginning. As the children learn to use the equipment and become familiar with it, then it is gradually replaced with more complicated items. At no time, regardless of the children's ability, should there be an excess of equipment crowded on the shelves so that the children cannot see what is available to them. Also, all items should be easily removed and returned to their proper place.

Each day during the Free Play or Choice Period the teacher will observe children using these materials. Sometimes she may interest them by talking or by assisting them in working with whatever they have selected. The teacher will also be able to learn more about individual children because so many items lend themselves to solitary involvement. At this time, for a few minutes, the teacher is able to give the child her undivided attention.

The daily reporting session gives the teacher another opportunity to find out if the children are using the equipment in the way they should and if learning is taking place. As the children report daily, the teacher will be given clues as to when new items should be added and when some of the available equipment needs to be removed.

As is the case with all activities, the teacher will learn valuable information about individual children that she will want to convey to parents during her conferences with them.

The equipment in this area may be enhanced and supplemented by teacher-made materials. These items are designed to teach certain concepts such as matching, classification, sounds of letters, visual discrimination, number sequence, and measurement. Through active involvement with the materials, the child gains an understanding of the relatedness of the items. Through repeated experience in the activity, he builds the concepts. Conversation with the teacher allows the child to tell about his experience, and

136878

the teacher has the opportunity to ask him questions and help him become aware of certain concepts and to clarify what he has observed intuitively.

The following are some suggestions for teacher-made materials.

Touching Box — Sensory Perception

Various pieces of materials such as fur, oilcloth, velvet, nylon net, or any kind of fabric placed in a box labeled "Touching Box" gives a child the opportunity to touch, feel, and examine, thus developing his sensory powers of feeling. Several familiar objects such as a pencil, crayon, piece of cotton, or ruler may be placed in a box, along with a small blindfold, as another touching activity. This involves two children; one wears the blindfold and has to identify the object, while the other child checks to see if the objects are correctly identified.

Rhyming Box — Auditory Discrimination

A rhyming game may be made by having six or seven pictures and objects that rhyme, for example a picture of a star and a small plastic jar, a picture of a house and a small rubber mouse. Swing and ring, man and pan are rhyming words that may be used. Objects and pictures should be placed in an attractive box with a rhyming picture and object on the cover of the box.

Big and Little Cards — Matching

Big and little cards may be placed in a box. Matching big and little picture postcards may be purchased in most card shops.

Commercial Card Games — Classifying

Card games such as Snap® or Animal Rummy® may be arranged to help the child classify things. These games contain six sets of pictures with four cards each. Six envelopes with a picture pasted on each can provide the container for the three other matching pictures.

Pegboard Town — Representation

If children grow tired of the usual pegs and pegboards, cut green kitchen sponges into small pieces and glue to the pegs to represent trees; supply small plastic cars and buildings so that roadways for the cars may be erected on the pegboards.

Clown and Ball Game — Motor Skills; One-to-One Correspondence

A wide-mouthed clown made from a round-shaped box can catch small rubber balls. This devise will enable two or three children to have a contest to see who can throw the greatest number of balls into the clown's mouth. Children may keep score by making a mark on paper each time the ball rolls in the clown's mouth.

Greeting Cards — Visual Interpretation; Language Development

A box of picture postcards and birthday and greeting cards make it possible for a child to enjoy interpreting pretty pictures. Children can be encouraged to talk about the cards during reporting time, giving them an opportunity to use language and name objects.

Sewing Box — Eye-Hand Coordination

A box containing different kinds of fabrics, lace, ribbon, bias tape, easy-cutting pinking scissors, thimble, needle, thread, pins, paper dress patterns, ready-cut garments, and dolls will offer children the opportunity to create with fabrics.

Picture Boxes — Matching*

This activity may be made by either drawing or pasting pictures on the inside lid of a hosiery box. Mount duplicate pictures on squares of cardboard. These may be matched to pictures on the lid and then housed inside the box. Several boxes should be available.

One book, entitled *Workjobs,*[†] is a rich resource of ideas and suggestions for teacher-made materials and activities for language and mathematics. For each of the activities, the explicit directions include instructions for use, with ideas for follow-up discussion. A large photograph of children involved in the activity enhances the directions. The author has also discussed activity-centered learning, establishing procedures and routines, record keeping, and introducing new workjobs.

---

*Kindergarten learning centers. Bellevue, Washington: Bellevue Public Schools, p. 11. This is only one of many excellent ideas that may be found in *Kindergarten Learning Centers.*
[†]Lorton, Mary Baratta. *Workjobs*, Reading, Massachusetts: Addison-Wesley Publishing Company, 1972.

Chapter 5

BLOCKS

HISTORY does not record when blocks obtained universal acceptance as play equipment for the young child. However, Froebel incorporated blocks into his gift series. Alphabet and picture blocks were considered essential toys in the late nineteenth century.

During the reform movement, the children used the blocks from Froebel's gifts to construct various objects. It was soon apparent to Patty Smith Hill that they needed larger blocks, so she designed Floor Blocks that provided for building on a large scale. They consisted of blocks of several lengths, which fit into grooved pillars, held together by iron bolts. With these blocks, houses, boats, and trains could be made large enough for a number of children to get inside. Not too long after the Hill Floor Blocks came into being, Caroline Pratt designed the unit blocks in present day common use but never patented them.

A unit block by definition is twice as wide as it is thick and twice as long as it is wide; all other blocks are either multiples or divisions of the unit or related to it in width, thickness, or length. In most sets a unit block measures 1 3/8 x 2 3/4 x 5 1/2.

Prior to entering a school situation, few if any children have had the opportunity to use unit blocks. So, for many children, blocks are a new and exciting medium of expression.

Blocks offer children opportunities to construct, to put things together, and to build. Children's creative block endeavors can range from a simple square to a complex village.

At first, the child experiments with blocks by stacking them, pushing them, or by making simple outline enclosures. Later the child becomes more adept at using the blocks, and he builds more complicated structures.

There are many mathematical concepts inherent in block play. Steven and Duane are working out the concept of size as Steven points to his construction and says, "My building is the biggest"; Duane counters this remark by saying, "My house is little, but I'll build the biggest house in the world."

Young children work with sizes, shapes, numbers, fractions, and solids while using blocks. Children feel and recognize size and shapes with their hands and bodies. Later they learn words that label. Children match these concepts and arrange and measure blocks. They notice likenesses and differences. As children build with blocks, they learn such concepts as more than, longer than, higher than, smaller than, over, under, in front of, beneath, half as big, and half as high. As we observe two boys playing with blocks, we might hear Terry say to Tony, "We need more blocks over here." Tony might answer, "We sure do, and put some under here," as he points to a tunnellike structure. It is essential that these experiences precede attempts at labeling the concepts. Block play supplies these necessary experiences.

Social studies concepts are inherent in children's block play. Children build about the world they know. A child several hundred miles from New York City used his imagination in building a structure to represent the Empire State Building after having seen a picture of it in the newspaper. This child also told a story about his construction, which the teacher recorded for him, and he proudly took the story home to read to his parents. After a group of five-year-olds had had several walks in the neighborhood, they began to construct buildings to represent the buildings in their environment. The teacher recognized this as an early form of a map and began to expand their understandings with pictures and real maps. Subsequent walks led to more complex structures with greater detail. In recreating their environment, these children had to communicate, exchange ideas, plan, and execute.

Scientific principles are also used in block building. The incline of a ramp makes it possible to roll a car from one level to another in the structure. When string is added to the available equipment, more complicated "machinery" appears, such as an elevator used to raise or lower materials. This can be made by wrapping one end of the string around a cylinder, and in some cases an actual pulley will be part of the equipment in the block area. Through block building children learn to observe, compare, classify, predict, and interpret.

The activity of block building promotes language expression. Children share ideas, and there is need to describe their block building endeavors to their peers and teacher. Labeling the buildings and streets of a village contributes to the child's awareness of signs and stimulates his interest in reading real signs outside of school.

While experiencing curriculum-related activities with blocks, young children are also developing physical skills. Eye-hand coordination is constantly put into practice in building. The evenness or unevenness of matching corners gives evidence of maturity of controls. Managing to carry three or more blocks without dropping them is a physical skill for many children. Esther Starks says that "when it comes to working in close proximity to other children or walking around several constructions on the way from the supply shelves to one's project, good physical coordination is indeed a requirement if the trip is to be accomplished without an accident."*

Children experience a tremendous amount of physical activity during block building sessions. The teacher should view this as supplement to otherwise inadequate opportunities for exercise in programs limited by time, space, and inclement weather.

Blocks are invaluable in helping children to develop socially. Taking turns and respecting the rights and ideas of others are social skills that blocks help to foster.

Esther B. Starks, in her booklet *Blockbuilding*, points out that blocks encourage social development because they contribute to the development of cooperative activity and desirable social habits.* She goes on to say that a young child begins working

---

*Starks, Esther. *Blockbuilding*. Washington, D.C.: American Association of Elementary-Kindergarten-Nursery Educators, 1970.

alone with blocks and is content with solitary play. Later, in parallel play, he plays with his blocks near another child, who is also playing with his own blocks. Seldom do the two come into contact. When they do, they have associative play; often it involves taking things away from each other. Finally, in the cooperative stage, children really work together, sharing ideas, blocks, and labor.

An adequate block supply should consist of a variety of shapes. The most popular ones are the larger, plain types (double and quadruple units), with a few ramps, triangles, cylinders, pillars, and arches to provide for variety and experimentation.

Figure 2 illustrates a suggested list of the types of blocks for young children to use in a classroom setting for a group of twenty-five five-year-olds.

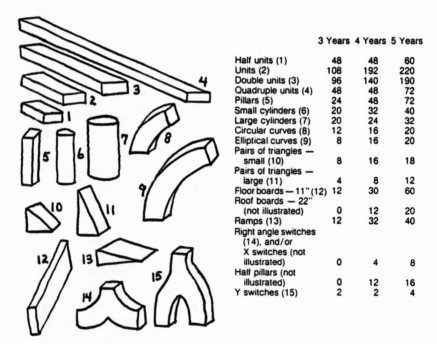

	3 Years	4 Years	5 Years
Half units (1)	48	48	60
Units (2)	108	192	220
Double units (3)	96	140	190
Quadruple units (4)	48	48	72
Pillars (5)	24	48	72
Small cylinders (6)	20	32	40
Large cylinders (7)	20	24	32
Circular curves (8)	12	16	20
Elliptical curves (9)	8	16	20
Pairs of triangles — small (10)	8	16	18
Pairs of triangles — large (11)	4	8	12
Floor boards — 11" (12)	12	30	60
Roof boards — 22" (not illustrated)	0	12	20
Ramps (13)	12	32	40
Right angle switches (14), and/or X switches (not illustrated)	0	4	8
Half pillars (not illustrated)	0	12	16
Y switches (15)	2	2	4

Figure 2. Suggested equipment for block building. A set of blocks for a group of fifteen to twenty children (numbers in parentheses refer to the drawing). From Jessie Stanton, Alma Weisberg, and the faculty of the Bank Street School for Children, *Play Equipment for the Nursery School* (New York: Bank Street College of Education). Used by permission.

A group of three- and four-years-olds need the same kind of blocks as fives but not as many of the variety of shapes.

The threes and fours should build with the units, double units, quadruple units, circular curves, and cylinders. However, as children gain mastery with these shapes, others should be added. Often in the early stages of block building, too many blocks can be overwhelming to three- and four-year-old children. This can also be true of five-year-old children if they have not had previous experience building with blocks. Thus, the number of blocks as well as the different shapes should be less for three, fours, and inexperienced fives.

Accessories to extend block play may consist of transportation toys, such as wooden and plastic cars, trucks, buses, fire trucks, boats, trains, and wagons; wood and rubber animals; and people representing various ages, ethnic groups, and occupations.

These accessories should be introduced a few at a time, but not until the children have had sufficient time to experiment with blocks. For some this may take four or five days, and for others it may take three or four weeks.

The booklet *Selecting Educational Equipment and Materials for Schools & Home** gives suggested lists of blocks and accessories as well as names and addresses of commercial companies from whom they can be purchased.

Adequate storage and a sufficient area in which to build are imperative for successful block building. The building area should be directly in front of or in close proximity to the storage shelves. The size of the room will dictate the amount of space to be used for building. Each child needs an area of at least three feet square to work in, and in a small room the block area may only accommodate three or four children.

The most suitable storage seems to be open shelving, which permits neatly stacked piles, and with enough partitions to allow separate sections for each type of blocks. Within each section a pattern of the block cut from construction paper, or painting on the shelf, or one of the real blocks glued to the shelf indicates the size and shape of the block that fits in the particular cubicle. In

---

*Association for Childhood Education International. *Selecting educational equipment and materials for schools & home.* Washington, D.C.: author, 1976, 108 pp.

all storage situations, the blocks should be easily and quickly put away by the children so that "clean up time" takes only a few minutes.

Often teachers do not permit children to play with blocks because of the noise factor. This author found that noise was a factor that affected block play in a negative way by reducing the amount of speech and curtailing construction.* When noise is a negative factor that influences block play, some thought should be given to the physical environment.

An alcove having walls and ceiling treated with sound-absorbent materials and a floor covered with thick carpeting or cork tiling would be the ideal setting for block building. In existing facilities, an area could be carpeted or covered with acoustical tiles.†

In a situation where no alcove or screening is used, marking the area with masking tape will supply the children with boundary lines for their structures and assist in the physical organization of the room. Once the teacher sets the stage by providing the raw materials (blocks and suitable accessories), adequate floor space, and time for building, she serves as a resource person and a guide to the children. Too often a teacher feels that after the stage is set that she is not needed. This is not true.

To give the children guidance the teacher makes frequent visits to the block area. Early in the year, children need help in matters of safety rules, in the carrying of blocks, the height of structures, and taking blocks in and out of the storage area. It also is imperative that children know that you do not throw blocks or walk on them.

Sometimes the teacher may quietly observe the children in their endeavors, or she may be a contributor. If a child is trying to make a tower or stack his blocks and is having difficulty, the teacher may make a suggestion to help him gain skill and mastery with the material and his activity. The teacher can show interest by favorable comments or asking questions. Cowe reported that

---

*Cowe, Eileen Grace. *A study of kindergarten activities for language development.* Unpublished doctoral dissertation, Teachers College, Columbia University, 1967, pp. 65, 66.

†R.H. Stone Products, 13735 Puritan, Detroit, Michigan 48227

questions asked by the researcher sparked conversation and more elaborate buildings were constructed.* She also says it would be wise for the teacher to make comments or ask questions that would help the children to describe, evaluate, and explain what they are doing.

As the teacher observes children using blocks, she will be aware of accessories and materials needed to enhance their constructions. For example, if children are trying to put a roof on the building, she could supply them with a piece of fabric or paper. Children laying out streets may need paper and felt-tipped markers for street signs.

If she observes a block tower or something resembling a wall, she might say, "Oh that reminds me of a poem," and then recite: "Blocks will build a tower tall. Blocks will make a long, long wall. Blocks will build a house or place, a truck, a tunnel, or a train. Get the blocks, so we can see what they'll build for you and me."†

Listening to the children's conversations and observing their structures may suggest to the teacher stories, poems, and songs related to their interests. A teacher read the story *The Boats on The River*‡ when the children needed clarification on different kinds of boats. The song "Automobile Ride"§ was enjoyed by the children after the teacher observed cars being constructed and children taking make-believe rides. While visiting the block area the teacher will get suggestions for certain kinds of pictures to be displayed. Many teachers have read the book *What Can We Do With Blocks?*‖ during story time and then placed it in the block area. They have found its illustrations to be a great source of stimulation to young builders.

---

*Cowe, Eileen Grace. *A study of kindergarten activities for language development.* San Francisco: R and E Research Associates, 1974, p. 30.

†Jacobs, Leland B. Professor Emeritus, Columbia University, New York, New York.

‡Flack, Marjorie. *The boats on the river.* New York: The Viking Press, 1946, 31 pp.

§Buttolph, Edna. *Music is motion.* Cincinnati, Ohio: The Willis Music Company, 1951, p. 18.

‖Shaine, Frances & Pru, Herric. *What can we do with blocks?* New York: Gosset & Dunlap, Inc. 1964.

A Polaroid® camera may be an unorthodox piece of equipment for the teacher to use when she visits the block area. However, taking pictures of the block constructions with a Polaroid camera dignifies the children's creative endeavors and gives them the opportunity to look at what they have done after the blocks are stored on the shelf. Teachers who have done this report that children build more elaborate and complex structures. Also, more cooperative play takes place, and children use language of a more complex nature. These picture records give children a sense of accomplishment and are a helpful reference for parent conferences.

A valuable resource on the use of blocks is the movie *Blocks — A Medium for Perceptual Learning.* * This movie skillfully portrays the use of blocks with young children. It presents mathematic and scientific concepts that children can learn while using blocks. It shows the various kinds of blocks that are available as well as convenient and adequate storage facilities. The narrator gives the teacher suggestions and techniques to help guide the children with block building activities. This movie is appropriate to show to parents and administrators.

The Block Book† covers all aspects of block building and gives both the inexperienced and the experienced teacher the philosophy as well as suggestions and techniques to use when young children build with blocks.

The teacher should keep a record of the children participating and should make sure each child has the opportunity to build with blocks. If children are left on their own without teacher guidance, the same children tend to utilize the blocks regularly while others never participate.

The teacher should be evaluating the progress of the children as they participate in block building. On her visits each day to the block area, she will be able to observe if more cooperative play is taking place, if the structures are more complex, and if the children are gaining control of the material. Another excellent way of evaluating students' progress is the oral report by each

---

*Campus Film Distributors Corp., 14 Madison Avenue, P.O. Box 206, Valhalla, New York 10595

†Hirsch, Elizabeth (Ed.). *The block book.* Washington, D.C.: NAEYC, 1974, 108 pp.

child during the daily reporting session.

As each child reports orally, the teacher should be aware of the child's ability to recall, explain, and answer questions about what he has done with the blocks during the Free Play or Choice Period.

Too often, teachers, particularly teachers of preschool and kindergarten children, view evaluations of children's progress as something that can only be done by using a paper-and-pencil test. Thus, they assume that these children cannot be evaluated. This is not true. The teacher's observations of each child during a reporting session is a valid and certainly an appropriate way of appraising the child's progress. It is imperative that a teacher consider the daily reporting session with a group of young children to be as important as a written assignment that an elementary teacher would give a group of fourth or fifth grade students.

The reporting session will also give the teacher clues as to when new material and equipment should be introduced. And finally, it will give her valuable information about each child that she will use during parent conferences. For example, Peter, who builds elaborate and complicated block structures, and is able to recall and describe them in great detail, demonstrates physical dexterity, organized thinking, and oral language facility. His block structures show the use of extensive imagination applied to problem-solving situations. The reporting of what he has done brings forth thinking about sequential procedure through which he has worked and makes use of elaborate speech. All of these developments help pave the way for learning to read. The teacher should make the parents aware of these benefits.

Occasionally a parent will say, "My child played with blocks when he was four years old in a day care center, and now he still has the same old blocks in the kindergarten." Often the parent is justified in a remark like this when developmental changes are not made in the conduct of the activities.

Block building in April should be different from block building in September. This will only take place if the teacher observes and guides the children so that block building becomes increasingly more challenging and continues to promote physical, social, emotional, and intellectual growth.

Chapter 6

HOUSEKEEPING

THE doll corner or housekeeping area has been a part of the scene in classrooms for young children since the late teens. In a speech to the kindergarten department of the NEA in 1919, Alice Temple was advocating home and community life experiences as part of the kindergarten curriculum.*

Having an area in the classroom where children could use child-sized domestic equipment represented a complete change from the Froebelian gifts and occupations. The intent of the innovative materials and equipment was not to supply knowledge but to offer children the opportunities to extend and organize experiences and to solve problems in familiar settings.

This area is often called the doll corner. However, "doll corner" is a term that may convey to parents and some administrators that very little learning, if any, is taking place. A more appropriate term is the housekeeping area.

The equipment and accessories for this area encourages dramatic play related to social studies. It can be a center for dramatizing the work of the many community helpers, such as the firefighter, the police officer, the mail carrier, the doctor, the repair person, the electrician, the plumber, and the grocer. When a child puts himself in the role of another person, what he does is imitate and interpret that person's actions. Through this process he gradually acquires a clearer understanding of himself and his world.

---

*Weber, Evelyn. *The kindergarten: Its encounter with educational thought in America.* New York: Teachers College Press, 1969, p. 93.

The housekeeping area provides a setting in which the children can socialize and communicate with each other, thus offering numerous possibilities for cooperative play.

As children use the equipment in the housekeeping area, they are developing their usage of language, enlarging their vocabularies, using their imagination, and thinking through situations.

This area should contain a child-sized table, chairs, cupboards, stove, sink, refrigerator, sofa or divan, rocking chair, dresser and full-length mirror, doll carriage, and doll beds, one of which should be of child size. In addition to this equipment, the area should be supplied with dolls of various sizes (preferably unbreakable) representing different ethnic groups, doll clothes, and such items as child-sized unbreakable dishes (representing both china and cooking utensils), telephone, grocery cart, broom and dustpan, iron and ironing board. Two leading manufacturers of this equipment are Childcraft Education Corporation* and Community Playthings.† Supplementary items may be contributed from homes: plastic soap bottles, cereal boxes, empty fruit and vegetable cans opened on the bottom and cleaned, and any realia that enhances the play in this area.

Stuff bread wrappers with newspapers and tape shut. Mount pictures of foods on heavy cardboard, then laminate or cover with adhesive clear plastic for use on plates. Also use TV dinner carton cut-outs for pretend food.‡ Dress-up clothes§ for both boys and girls and accessories such as hats, purses, belts, shoes, and jewelry may be included.

In the beginning, too many items in the housekeeping area can be overwhelming to the average child. There is a tendency for him to pick up one thing after another, as his eyes fall upon so many objects, that he fails to focus his attention upon using

---

*Childcraft Education Corp., 20 Kilmer Road, Edison, New Jersey 08817

†Community Playthings, Rifton, New York 12471

‡Flemming, Bonnie Mack, Hamilton, Darlene Softley and Hicks, JoAnne Deal. *Resource For Creative Teaching In Early Childhood Education.* New York: Harcourt Brace Jovanovich, 1977, p. 550.

§ Adult clothes may need to be altered slightly for the children. Women's dresses may have much too large a neckline. They should be adjusted in some way to more nearly fit the child. Dresses may be so long that they impede walking. In such cases, they should be shortened. Blouses and shirts may be more adaptable to children of various sizes. Men's adult clothing in the smaller sizes are a better choice than those of medium and large size. Jackets may need the sleeves shortened. Trousers and pants are not appropriate because they are too cumbersome to put on over the children's clothes.

anything. To avoid this aimless behavior, the contents of the housekeeping area should at first be limited to minimum essentials such as bed, doll, doll clothes, table, chairs, cupboard, and dishes. In two or three days, add the stove, refrigerator, more doll clothes, another doll, and rocking chair. Continue to add furniture and accessories over a two week period until all of the standard equipment for the housekeeping area has been introduced. Then gradually add the supplementary items. They will enhance the activities and spark the imagination of the children using it.

Whenever new items are added to the area, the teacher may wish to introduce them to the entire group, having a discussion as to their use and care. At other times, particularly when such discussions are unneeded, the items may simply be placed within the area to serve as a small surprise for the children.

The standard equipment for this area should be arranged so that it gives the impression of at least two rooms. Small rugs will help to curtail the noise as well as giving the appearance of a well-furnished house. The arrangement may be such that a false window can be made with curtains of fabric or crepe paper.

The housekeeping furniture should be arranged in such a way that walking into the area gives the illusion of walking into a house. Dividers that define the area enhance this illusion. In addition to those manufactured specifically for this purpose, one may be able to secure dividers locally. Department stores often set up room displays for a period of time, using dividers, which are subsequently discarded. Frequently these attractive dividers can be secured for the asking.

A unique way of creating privacy for the area is to suspend strips of twisted ribbon, heavy paper, or rope from hooks in the ceiling to a board secured to the floor. The booklet *Arranging the Informal Classroom** gives directions for making various screens and dividers. Regardless of what is used to define the area, it should allow the teacher to see what is taking place within it.

---

*Engel, Brenda S. *Arranging the informal classroom.* Newton, Massachusetts: Education Development Center, Inc., 1973, pp. 46-50.

The author found that a greater amount and more complex speech took place in the housekeeping area that was partially set off from the rest of the classroom with screens that afforded an at-home privacy.*

A teacher who did not have the screens got the same effect by rearranging the furniture.† She moved the refrigerator, cupboard, and sink to a position that formed a wall. With the old arrangement the children would run out of the area, scattering the dishes and doll clothes through the classroom. With the new arrangement the children stayed in the housekeeping area, and more constructive play took place.·

Another teacher closed the housekeeping area to permit entrance from only one side.‡ This cut down on the traffic between the block area and the book corner. More constructive play emerged, changing the tone of the room.

The teacher makes frequent visits to the area during Free Play or Choice Period as a resource person and guide. Sometimes the teacher will be an observer, and sometimes she may be an active participant, sharing a pretend cup of tea. These visits will give her cues and ideas about items to enhance and extend the activities that are taking place. As she quietly observes, she may discover that more doll clothes and blankets are needed, or more dress-up clothes should be available, perhaps a nurse's cap or a doctor's kit if the children are assuming these roles, or she may get cues for selecting certain stories to be read at story time. For example, children who are pretending to make soup will enjoy *Stone Soup*§ or *Chicken Soup and Rice.*‖ Perhaps the teacher can arrange to have the children make real soup in the classroom. If children are pretending to make cookies, the supply of Play-Doh® modeling compound may be placed in the refrigerator so that the pretend baking of cookies will be more realistic. Cookbooks similar to

---

*Cowe, Eileen Grace. *A study of kindergarten activities for language development.* Unpublished doctoral dissertation, Teachers College, Columbia University, 1967, p. 161.

†Murray, Diane. ABC Child Care, Queens, New York.

‡Kriegsman, Robbyn. Children's School, Saint Anthony, New York, New York.

§Brown, Marcia. *Stone soup.* New York: Charles Scribner's Sons, 1947.

‖Sendak, Maurice. *Chicken soup and rice.* Evanston, Illinois: Harper & Row, 1962.

*The A to Z No Cook Cookbooks** and *The Seabury Cook Book for Boys and Girls*[†] or recipe cards with illustrated directions may be placed in the kitchen area.

A copy of the book *Costumes For You To Make*[‡] may be placed near the dress-up clothes. The pictures in this book may stimulate ideas and innovative ways to use the clothing and other accessories.

Listening to the children's conversation while they are playing in this area may provide a cue for certain trips that will extend and clarify some of their thinking. An example might be a trip to a bakery, grocery store, or fruit and vegetable market if conversations seem to center around foods and cooking.

Observing and listening to individual children playing house roles will give the teacher information that might not be learned in any other situation. A very quiet, shy child may suddenly take on the role of a busy, important mother, ordering people around and telling them what to do. Incidents like this will aid the teacher in guiding this child.

The teacher may observe a child telling a story to another child or to a doll. This incident can be reported to the parent, explaining that this is a form of reading.

The teacher's frequent visits to this area will help her evaluate the children's ability to use the equipment properly and with more sophistication. She will observe the children's ability to get along with each other, noting those who may have some difficulty.

Besides the contribution to the child's overall language development, the reporting session provides an opportunity for both the teacher and the children to consider the activities that have taken place in the housekeeping area.

---

*Lambardi, Felipe Rojas. *The A to Z no cook cookbook.* New York: Creations, Inc., 1972.

[†]Moore, Eva. *The Seabury cook book for boys and girls.* New York: The Seabury Press, 1969, 48 pp.

[‡]Purdy, Susan. *Costumes for you to make.* New York: J.B. Lippincott Company, 1971, 121 pp.

Chapter 7

LIBRARY AREA

THE book corner or classroom library has long been a part of the scene in a pre-kindergarten or kindergarten room. The book *First Experiences with Literature** gives the details about setting up a library corner within the classroom. In today's classroom libraries you will also find audiovisual material and equipment.

When books are a part of the daily activities of the classroom, it encourages children to browse. As they browse they will see that there are many kinds of books — different stories, different kinds of pictures, and different sizes of books. During browsing periods, children may develop a respect and a technique of handling books, even though they do not read. If after reading a book to the children the teacher places it in the library area, members of the class will often seek out that particular one because of their familiarity with its content.

The area may be used as a research place and will give the children a fund of general information. For example, children may bring in some article such as a flower, rock, leaf, shell, plant, or some item they want to know about. They can be referred to picture books showing these articles in colorful form. When the child identifies a comparable picture of the article, the teacher reads what the pages say.

When records and tapes are available it encourages children to listen to good stories and music. On the surface, this may appear to be purely enjoyment, but as they are enjoying it, they are de-

---

*Dalgliesh, Alice. *First experiences with literature.* New York: Charles Scribner's Sons, 1932, 162 pp.

ıg listening skills. It gives them something to talk about, .f someone asks them to tell the story, they must recall a seq.ıence of events. Listening to stories and telling them call forth the same thinking processes and use the same comprehension skills that reading does. Consistent use of storytelling and discussion based on the content of books and recordings provides a valuable base for the use of language in a way that ideally prepares the child for reading and working with books.

A child may record on tape his stories or perceptions of certain books or recordings, thus giving him the opportunity to experiment with language and have fun with it.

Children may enjoy vicarious experiences from books and recordings which will stimulate interest and help them see themselves as persons who can enjoy exploring language and learning to read. All of the activities in this area should help to make the child aware of the printed word and to develop a desire to read it.

The equipment for this area is a table, chairs, rug, books, bookshelves, records, record player, story tapes, tape recorders, sound filmstrips, and an automatic rear screen sound projector. There should also be shelves, racks, or small baskets for storing tapes, records, and filmstrips.

This area should be distinctive and inviting. If the table used can be quite different from the other tables in the room, this alone will make the library area a very special place. A round table may be used, thus making a very definite contrast to the square or oblong tables used for other purposes. Foster and Headley* suggest a hexagonal table, as it seems to give more space for opening out the large picture books. It is desirable also to have the chairs used in this area be distinctive. If it is not possible to purchase new and different ones, then the addition of slip-back covers (like a pillowcase) and seat covers or small cushions of attractive material, either cloth or plastic, will give the chairs a distinctive appearance. The area may be equipped with one or two child-sized armchairs and a rocking chair. A small attractive rug will add warmth and charm to the place.

---

*Foster, Josephine C. & Headley, Neith. *Education in the kindergarten* (2nd ed.). New York: American Book Company, 1948, p. 203.

There must be a place to store books. A low bookcase with open shelves is usually very inviting. The shelves of a bookcase should never be "filled" with books because too many books makes it difficult for the children to locate one that captures their attention. Locating the desired book in a filled bookcase is a complicated problem when one cannot read and can see only the spine of the book. Keeping only ten or twelve books on a shelf that could hold as many as thirty enables the children to find a book with ease. Some of the books will be standing and others lying flat on the shelf, but it should be possible to take any book from the shelf without upsetting the whole order. Variations in shelf heights will help children keep books of similar size together, and a few upright partial partitions or bookends in the shelves will be a further aid to organization and will help to teach the children to classify books according to size.

Foster and Headley state that at first the number of books in the entire bookcase will probably not exceed fifteen or twenty. As the year progresses and the interests of the group develop, more and more books will be added. Some books that are seasonal in their interest will be on the shelves for a few days or a few weeks at most; others, as they are added, will remain on the shelves for the rest of the school year. According to Foster and Headley, the number on the shelves at any one time should not exceed thirty-five.*

This area may include both the record player and the tape recorder, which should be equipped with earphones so that some children can listen to records and tapes while others enjoy the books. Multiple jack boxes allow two or more children to listen to the same recording. A rear screen sound projector is another valuable piece of equipment for the area. This type has a self-contained screen, like a television set. Individual children or a small group with headphones can enjoy sound filmstrips on their own, after the teacher has loaded the machine. Two companies that manufacture this type of equipment with various sized screens are

---

*Foster, Josephine C. & Headley, Neith. *Education in the kindergarten* (4th Ed.). New York: Van Nostrand Reinhold Co., 1966, p. 226.

Dukane* and Singer.[†] Only a few records, tapes, and sound film-strips should be available at any one time. Records and tapes may be added a few at a time.

Books lists and book reviews to aid the teacher in selecting books for the classroom appear in bookstores, educational magazines, and libraries. Two excellent examples are *Bibliography of Books for Children*[‡] and *Books in Pre-School.*[§] The Bowmar Company[‖] is an excellent source of recorded music. Taylor Associates[¶] and Western Woods** are two leading producers of sound filmstrips of young children's books. The Taylor Associates TELL ME A STORY libraries and 10 word book/AV Ensembles are excellent materials to use in this area. A unique feature that encourages storytelling is a Tell-Back Booklet, a sheet of paper that when folded, forms a booklet containing nine line drawings depicting the key events in the story. These serve as notes for story-telling, assisting the child in recalling events in sequence, in more detail than he would remember on his own.

During Free Play or Choice Period, the teacher makes frequent visits to this area. In the beginning the children may need help in matters of handling a book and in turning the pages. They also should be encouraged to exercise judgment as to when their hands are or are not clean enough to handle material. When children have finished looking and using the materials, they may be expected to return them to their proper places. Loud conversations, hoarding books or recordings, and unnecessary moving about should be discouraged.

The teacher may quietly observe and listen, or she may be a contributor. She may suggest a certain book to a child. The teacher may ask questions about the stories or recordings the

---

*Dukane Corporation, 2900 Dukane Drive, St. Charles, Illinois 60174

[†]Singer Education Systems, 3750 Monroe Avenue, Rochester, New York 14603

[‡]Association for Childhood Education International, 3615 Wisconsin Avenue, N.W., Washington, D.C. 20016, 1980.

[§]National Association for the Education of Young Children, 1834 Connecticut Avenue, N.W., Washington, D.C. 20009, n.d.

[‖]Bowmar Company, 4563 Colorado Blvd., Los Angeles, California 90039

[¶]Taylor Associates, 10 Stepar Place, Huntington Station, New York 11746

**Western Woods, Weston, Connecticut 06880

children are using.

These visits will give her cues as to when new and different kinds of materials are needed. The teacher should be evaluating the children's progress as they use this area. On her visits each day she will be able to observe how the children handle the books, how carefully they look at the pictures, and if they are able to tell a story from the pictures.

This author found that a child whom the teacher had labeled nonverbal, when encouraged by an adult, eagerly told a story from the pictures of a book.* Most of the speech was composed of complete sentences — the type linguists would call complex. In a conversation with the teacher, it was ascertained that the story had not been read aloud in the classroom and that the child did not have the book at home. Here was a situation in which the child was able to tell a story from a book when she had pictures that stimulated her and an audience that gave her attention.

The oral report by each child during the daily reporting session is another opportunity for the child to develop his language and to help the teacher ascertain his progress in his thinking and use of language.

---

*Cowe, Eileen Grace. *A study of kindergarten activities for language development.* Unpublished doctoral dissertation, Teachers College, Columbia University, 1967, p. 126.

Chapter 8

ART MEDIA

ART is an integral part of the entire school curriculum. It is a means through which a child can express his feelings in a satisfying way. As he practices using art media, he gradually becomes aware of the variations of his products. This is one type of visual discrimination, a skill that has many applications beyond the art projects. For example it is one of the principal skills in learning to read.

The use of art materials helps to develop eye-hand coordination, which will be equally important in learning to write. Art experiences encourage the child to rely upon his own way of expressing things. The continued opportunity to make selections and judgments, to experiment and to solve problems in an individual way, gives the child a pattern of approach in other learning situations.

Working with art media helps develop personal sensitivity and reliance on one's own taste and judgment. Using manual abilities and expressing feelings and ideas with different materials counterbalances some of the verbalization and factual learning of other areas. Creative work gives a sense of personal satisfaction and confidence. There is sensory tactile and emotional satisfaction in handling and manipulating materials. Children learn the practicality of a well-organized work space and convenient storage of materials. They learn to assume the responsibility for cleaning up and putting materials away.

Crayons of various colors should be available. They may be kept in boxes of eight colors or separated according to colors and put in small boxes painted to match the crayons they hold.

An easel is certainly not essential for painting, but it does afford the child an experience that he usually has not had at home. Children may work at tables or on the floor. In such instances, paints may be conveniently placed in tote trays. An excellent arrangement is to use the wire tote trays or holders for drinking glasses. Soft drink cardboard carriers are also useable. Plastic cups may hold individual colors of paint.

Using a carrier on a flat surface may be even better for some children. So often they fill their brushes with excessive amounts of paint, which drips down the picture on an easel.

Paint used by young children should be opaque in quality. Poster paint comes in either powder or liquid form.

A brush for each jar of paint should be provided. If the handles of the paintbrushes are painted to match the color of paint in which they are used, the child will be encouraged to dip his brush always in the same color of paint. Brushes (of assorted sizes and shapes) may be kept in a large tin can or plastic bucket near the easel or paint carrier. Clean brushes should be placed in the container heads up and handles down.

Smocks should be available. Each child may have his own, or several may be shared.

Both construction and poster paper in 9 x 12 sheets and 12 x 18 should be available. Construction paper is heavier than poster paper and may be used for many activities. It cuts easier and absorbs less paste than poster paper. Poster paper lends itself to folding and tearing.

Manila paper should be available in buff, gray, and white. It is especially satisfactory for crayon work. Manila paper may be purchased in 12 x 18 inch sheets. If smaller paper is needed, these pieces may be folded and cut.

Newsprint is suitable for painting. The white sheets in an 18 x 24 inch size seem to be suitable for day-by-day use. Paper should be stored on shelves with only a small supply available. Children should not be expected to take paper from a large stack or pile.

Clay should be available and stored in a plastic container. Clay boards should be used for clay work. They may be purchased from any of the companies that sell art supplies. Play-Doh modeling compound is a material that is excellent for those who are in the manipulative or symbolic stage of modeling. Play-Doh may be purchased commercially, or a homemade substitute may be used.

Pencils, varying in size from the large soft-lead pencils to a size the teacher may be using, are essential.

Felt-tipped markers should be available in boxes containing a variety of colors.

Both blunt and semi-pointed scissors should be available. Sometimes scissors are kept in covered cardboard or wooden boxes into which holes that exactly fit the point of the scissors have been drilled.

A small clothes bar makes an excellent rack to hang paintings on while they are drying.

All of these materials are introduced early in the school year. Crayons may be used the first day, as they take little skill to use and many children have had experience with them prior to entering school. Pencils should be available from the first day, and children may use them instead of crayons. Like crayons some children will have used them at home.

Painting with tempera paints may be introduced two or three weeks after the school year has started. Painting materials are presented to children, and they are told the importance of putting a smock on while painting. The teacher should demonstrate the use of the brush, showing how to drag a loaded brush across the inside of the jar to remove excess paint. Also the teacher instructs them to keep a separate brush in each jar of paint so as not to mix colors. Perhaps two or three colors of paint may be introduced at first and then the others gradually added over a period of three or four weeks. In the first session, cleanup procedures should be explained and the children told where to place their paintings for drying.

Scissors are necessary equipment for many art activities. If children find it difficult to cut with scissors, they should be encouraged to open the scissors wide and attempt to cut close to the screw that jams the two blades. This lessens the danger of the paper slipping between the blades. The child can also learn to pull the material to be cut towards himself and at the same time to push the scissors away from himself; his cutting efforts will meet with greater success if this is done.

Modeling compound (Play-Doh or homemade) may be introduced about two or three weeks after school has started. After the children have worked with modeling compound for four or five weeks, clay may be introduced. After the introduction of clay, modeling compound should still be available. When the teacher introduces modeling compound or clay, she takes a piece and shows it can be pushed, punched, and pulled into a shape, always being careful not to make a finished product. The children should use a clay board or heavy paper for their modeling endeavors. Children should be told what to do with modeled forms, where to put the clay or compound after use, and to wipe up the table or floor with a wet sponge.

To give the children guidance the teacher makes frequent visits to the area where children are using art media. Early in the year it is important that the teacher praise the child for his efforts and correct use of the materials. The teacher does not criticize the way the child paints. For example, a teacher would never give a model of a tree and have a child copy it. However, at some other time the teacher makes it possible for the children to look at trees and discuss how they grow, the bigness of the trunk, how the branches spread out, how leaves group themselves around the branches. As children become aware of things, they gradually and slowly include this awareness in their paintings. On her visits, the teacher will get cues as to the kinds of opportunities she should provide for the children in order to afford this type of development and growth.

Paintings and modeling endeavors should be displayed in the room, and over a period of time each child should be represented, regardless of the stage of his development.

Children enjoy showing their paintings and their modeled objects and telling about them, and this will take place during the daily reporting session. As each child reports orally, the teacher should be aware of the child's ability to tell about his paintings and his modeled objects. The child can name and point out the different colors he has used. The children may be encouraged to tell stories about their endeavors. The element of fantasy in a child's art and storytelling encourage the use of the imagination.

Chapter 9

WATER PLAY

WATER play became part of the curriculum during the early days of the Kindergarten reform, and it continues to be recognized as a worthwhile activity for young children. But in spite of this, water play has never been given a conspicuous place in programs for young children. Perhaps some teachers feel that it is too messy and do not realize the learning implications inherent in it.

Water play is utterly fascinating to young children. It is a rare child who does not love to dabble in water. Most children spend more time at the sink than is necessary for efficient washing. They always walk through the puddles, never around them. They love to pour water back and forth into containers of different sizes and shapes, and they never seem to tire of floating toy boats or ducks on its surface. In addition to being delightful, relaxing, and joyous, water play is a vehicle for developing the concepts of mathematics and science.

Children can learn the properties of water through play. By pouring water into various containers, it can be shown that it takes the shape of the object into which it is poured, round, square, etc. When water is not in a container, it has no specific shape, but it runs and spreads. Water absorbs, evaporates, and freezes. It can act with force and push things away. It has weight and volume, and some things float on it while others cannot. Substances of different color or texture can be mixed with water. Flour and salt may be mixed with it to make modeling compound; mixed with tempera it makes paint; mixed with soap, it makes bubbles. They can also learn that a function of water is that it cleans.

As children experience the many and varied water play activities, they are observing, discovering, reasoning, questioning, and experimenting. While doing this, most children converse with each other, thus giving many opportunities for language development. The activities of water play offer children the opportunity to engage in solitary, parallel, or cooperative play, and it demands no special skills from the children.

Suggested equipment may be a sink or large galvanized or plastic tub, several measuring cups, egg beaters, sieves, lengths of hose, soapsuds, ladles, plastic bottles, jugs and containers of various sizes and shapes (many of equal volume) plastic squeeze bottles, and plastic syringes.

Dorothy M. Hill says that different experiences are more apt to happen when different accessories are available. She has suggested that activity or participation kits be made up ahead of time and placed on open shelves ready for use.* An example is a bubble blowing kit containing a bottle full of bubble solution of 3/4 cup of liquid soap, 1/4 cup of glycerine or sugar, and 2 quarts of warm water. In addition to the bubble solution, include store-bought bubble pipes and plastic straws. Pipe cleaners, toothpicks, and plasticine clay should be available to make bubble frames; sponges, styrofoam cups, and small containers (plastic and metal) opened at both ends, should be in the kit, as well as terry cloth towels (small scrap pieces) for wiping up. Kits may be assembled for such activities as floating, measuring, washing toys, and bathing dolls.

Most equipment for water play is relatively inexpensive and easily obtainable. Childcraft Education Corporation† has excellent water play equipment. One outstanding piece of equipment is the Childcraft Sand and Water Play Table. It is an ideal classroom facility for both water and sand play. This heavy-duty table has a tough, durable trough of white ABS plastic, which is waterproof and abrasion resistant. A durable plastic spigot permits water to be emptied quickly and easily; casters on legs make it easy to move.

*Hill, Dorothy M. *Mud, sand and water.* Washington, D.C.: NAEYC, 1977.

†Childcraft Education Corp., 20 Kilmer Road, Edison, New Jersey 18817

The table has a wood top cover, which provides an extra work space when the sand and water table is not in use.

Waterproof poncho-type plastic aprons (used shower curtains cut with pinking shears) easily accessible to the children provide the necessary protection for water play.

Most of the equipment must be stored in locations where the children may reach it without adult assistance. Too much material available too soon may easily be overwhelming and chaotic to many children. A gradual introduction of materials by the teacher over an extended period of time is necessary. Because water play requires extra work in setting up the equipment and a fair amount of space in order to have a profitable experience, it may be offered intermittently throughout the year. In places where there is a great deal of cold wet weather it would not be as appropriate as it would be in areas of warm dry weather.

The teacher sets the stage by providing the equipment and supplies for water play, and then she serves as a guide to the children. This guidance is given by frequent visits to the area during the Free Play or Choice Period. Early in the year, children may need help in matters of safety rules regarding keeping the materials and the activity in the designated area. It is imperative that the children do not squirt water on each other.

The teacher listens to the children's lively conversations of fantasy, to recapture it later during the story, poetry, or music period. For example, the poem "Soap Bubbles"* may be used after the children have been blowing bubbles. Sometimes the teacher may quietly observe the children in their endeavors, or she may be a contributor. The teacher may make suggestions to help the children gain skill and mastery with the material and the activity. She can also show interest by asking questions. The teacher should keep records of the children participating so that all children will have this experience.

A valuable resource on the use of water play is the movie *Water Play For Teaching Young Children.*† This movie skillfully portrays young children engaged in water play. It presents the

---

*Allen, Marie Louise. *A pocketful of poems.* New York: Harper & Row Publishers, 1957, p. 28.

†New York University Film Library, 26 Washington Place, New York, New York, 10003

learning implications available to children when participating in this activity. It shows various kinds of materials, both commercial and "scrounge or good junk" that may be supplied by the parents or costs little or nothing. The narrator gives the teacher suggestions and techniques to help guide the children while engaged in water play.

One teacher, after seeing this film, said, "I not only received many wonderful ideas for water play, but I became aware of the fact that I should be more actively involved with the children, then I was able to say no to wild behavior that sometimes occurs."*

The book *Mud, Sand, and Water*† covers various aspects of using these materials with children.

An issue of *First Teacher*‡ entitled "Water For Fun and Learning" gives many excellent ideas and suggestions for things for young children to do with water.

On her visits to the area, the teacher evaluates the progress of the children by observing their use of the equipment and their ability to understand the scientific and mathematical concepts. Another excellent way of evaluating students' progress is the oral report by each child during the daily reporting session. As each child reports orally, the teacher should be aware of the child's ability to recall, explain, and answer questions about his experiences with water.

The daily reporting sessions and the teacher's visits to the area may give clues as to when new material and equipment could be introduced. It will also give her valuable information about each child that she will use during parent conferences. For example, Robyn, who discovers that water takes the shape of its container, demonstrates the ability to observe and to think. Her parents should be advised of her ability and how this will lead to future academic success.

---

*Kriegsman, Robbyn, Children's School, Saint Anthony, New York City.
†Hill, Dorothy M., *Mud, sand and water*. Washington, D.C.: NAEYC, 1977.
‡*First Teacher*, Volume 1, No. 7, 60 Main Street, Bridgeport, Conn.

Chapter 10

SAND PLAY

THE early publications of the curriculum reform at the Horace Mann Kindergarten list activities and the equipment for sand play. In spite of this, many preschool programs never offer this activity.

Sand play for young children is enjoyable and satisfying. Children may pat, poke, pile, and pound sand. Some children never tire of pouring sand back and forth from one container to another.

Sand play, like water play, provides opportunities for children to experience mathematics and science activities. As the children play with sand, they soon discover the properties of sand. They observe that it takes the shape of the container into which it is poured. It spreads and can act as a force. It has weight and volume. When water is added to it, it can be shaped and formed. It can be molded and patted into positions that will hold their shape, so mountains, caves, lakes, rivers, tunnels, wells, subways, etc. can be made successfully.

As children use sand, they are observing, discovering, reasoning, questioning, and experimenting. Children can converse with each other as they play with sand, giving them an opportunity to use language. They may engage in solitary, parallel, or cooperative play, and, like water, sand demands no special skills from the children.

A sand table or sandbox is imperative for sand play. It is advisable to have a cover for the table; when covered, it provides an additional space for work. The sand and water table sold by Childcraft Equipment (described in Chapter 9) is an excellent versatile piece of equipment.

Other equipment needed may be measuring cups, sieves, sifters, funnels, and a pair of balance scales. Dump trucks, bulldozers, and cars of a variety of sizes (depending on the size of the sand table), may also be used. It is wise to have a brush or broom and dustpan to clear up the spillings that are bound to occur.

The equipment must be stored where the children can reach it without adult assistance. Basically the same type of equipment is needed for sand as for water, but if both are being used at the same time, the equipment should be stored and labelled separately. A gradual introduction of the equipment by the teacher over an extended period of time is advisable. The size of the sandbox will determine the number of children it can accommodate and whether it can be offered on a daily basis or intermittently throughout the year.

Guidance is given by the teacher as she makes frequent visits to the area. When sand play is first introduced, the children will need help in the matters of confining the play to the area. It is imperative that children know that they are not allowed to throw sand at their peers or on the floor.

The teacher listens to the children's conversations for cues as to when other equipment should be added and how she may enhance their experiences through trips, music, or literature. The teacher may observe quietly or be a contributor by asking questions and/or making suggestions. As the teacher visits this area, she will observe whether they are gaining the mathematical and scientific concepts that can be experienced with sand.

As each child gives his report during the daily reporting session, the teacher can evaluate the children's progress. As the child tells about his experiences, the teacher will observe his ability to communicate to his classmates his concept of what he is doing. These reports may alert her to introduce new equipment.

Chapter 11

SHORT-TERM ACTIVITIES

SHORT-TERM activities, an important component of the Free Play or Choice Time, should be introduced as soon as the children have settled into the basic activities. This will probably be two or three weeks after their introduction.

Short-term activities are most often art activities or manipulative tasks related to curriculum areas or special events. Holidays and trips are occasions that spark interest in such activities.

Short-term activities uniquely prepare the kindergartener for the formal pencil-and-paper activities that comprise so much of his future schooling. They involve using paper, pencil, crayons, scissors, and paste. The manipulation of these materials develop the eye-hand coordination required in writing. It also encourages attention to small details, a skill needed in learning to read.

Also, the child is given a task involving the use of materials according to specific instructions. The assignment takes a period of time, and the child is expected to produce a finished product.

Children who have functioned in a classroom where they have learned to work independently for periods of time will be better prepared to assume the responsibilities of a learner in a more formal setting of first grade instruction. A short-term activity will involve only three to six children each day and will be offered for four to six days. In most instances, a new activity may be introduced every five or six days. Many of the short-term activities will be done by all of the children, others by only those who select them because of interest or maturity. These activities should be so simple that once the directions are given, little or no assistance is needed. At no time should the activity be so difficult that an adult must do any part of it.

In the beginning, the activities should require two or three steps and be done in one period. As the year progresses, they become more complicated, involving four or five steps and requiring two or three days to complete. First, the teacher should introduce the activity to the whole group. Then, the few children who will do the new activity are selected, while the others select one of the regularly functioning basic activities.

Many teachers make the mistake of trying to manage the entire class in doing a project at the same time. Such management requires the children to be patient and wait for the teacher or assistant to help them. This is expecting too much of children. While waiting for help, the children lose interest and often engage in unacceptable behavior such as excessive talking, noisemaking, moving about, and improperly using materials. In trying to keep the children in some kind of order, the teacher tells them to sit down and keep still for five or ten minutes while she helps another child. Pre-kindergarten and kindergarten children should not be expected to wait patiently for periods with nothing to do. Implementing short-term activities for only a few children per day eliminates such problems. When children work in small groups, the teacher has the opportunity to observe, study, and assist each one as needed.

One of the easiest short-term activities is Buttermilk Painting. Buttermilk is placed in a small (3 inch) foil pan, from which it is spread onto manila drawing paper, 12 x 18 inches, with a pastry brush.* Foil pans and pastry brushes can be purchased where kitchenware is sold. When the entire surface of the paper is covered with buttermilk, use large colored chalk for drawing pictures or designs. The completed picture should remain flat until dry. The buttermilk serves as a fixative and makes drawing with chalk a delightful experience.

A simple demonstration of the activity should be given to the whole group. However, the teacher does not make a finished picture; she simply shows how the buttermilk is spread on the

---

*Buttermilk will keep for several days without being refrigerated. If it gets thick, just add water.

paper and how the chalk is used. Buttermilk may be something new to some children, so a very brief explanation should be given.

After the demonstration, tell the children that three or four may do this, and ask for volunteers. Select the children who will do it the first day. If many children show great interest in this activity, assure them that they will have a turn another day and that only four can do it this time. Then proceed to assist the other children in making selections from among the previously established activities.

Prior to the demonstration of buttermilk painting, have an area set aside in which the children will work. It may be a table or a designated area on the floor. Pans of buttermilk, brushes, paper, and chalk should be available for each child so that he takes the materials and begins his painting immediately.

Assistance should not be given unless the children are not following directions. They may need encouragement to moisten the entire sheet of manila drawing paper before using the chalk. After the teacher has seen that the children are using the materials correctly, she should leave them. She checks back in five minutes to see if they are progressing according to her original directions. She makes the needed suggestions and compliments the children on what they are doing right. Then she leaves and checks back in a few more minutes.

The following day, the teacher explains, and demonstrates for the whole class again, how to do buttermilk painting. It is possible that some of the children who did buttermilk painting the first day may be able to help the teacher give the explanation. The second explanation should be very brief and to the point. Then, four different children should be selected to do it while others engage in the basic activities. The scheduling of four children per day for the short-term activity continues until all of the children have had the opportunity to engage in it.

Throughout the year activities are introduced and scheduled in a like manner. First, the presentation is made by the teacher to the whole group, and each day, three or four children do it until all have had an opportunity. After five or six days, another activity is introduced. It may be another art activity, or it could be an activity in any of the curriculum areas.

For example, in the area of science, the activity could be experimentation with the traveling of sound.* Have the children make a toy telephone, demonstrating that sound can be transmitted or that it travels through a material such as string. Punch a hole with scissors or a stick into the bottoms of two paper cups. Take a piece of string about 3 to 5 feet long and put it through the holes in the cups, then tie a knot in each end or tie a piece of paper to each end, making the ends so they will not come out of the hole. Some children may need assistance. One cup is held to the mouth of the speaker and the other cup is held to the ear of the listener so that imaginary telephone conversations may take place.

Prior to introducing this activity, focus the children's attention on a classroom sound. Have some children recall various sounds. Have one child leave the room and knock on the door. Ask "Can you see him?" "Can you hear him?" "If we can hear him, what is the sound doing?" For a very few minutes, continue with the discussion until the children realize that sound travels. Then proceed to give directions on how to make the telephone. Keep in mind that a presentation like this is very short, and directions for making the telephone should be simple. Children will be more creative in their telephone conversations if the teacher does not demonstrate. The four people who choose to do this activity will engage in telephone conversations after they have made their own telephone.

Each day four children will have a turn until each child has his own telephone. On successive days, as this activity is presented, involve the children who have already made telephones when giving the necessary directions. Such an activity presents the concept that sound travels and that sound can be transmitted through a string. This is an example of what Bruner must have meant when he said, "that any subject can be taught to any child in some honest form."†

---

*Jacobson & Cowe, Eileen G. *Beginning science.* New York: American Book Co., 1966. This book consists of many science activities for young children.

†Bruner, Jerome S. *The process of education.* Cambridge, Massachusetts: Harvard University Press, 1960, p. 52.

Each day while the children are purposely pursuing the activity, the teacher and the assistant teacher, if she has one, should move quietly and inconspicuously from child to child to observe and to see if assistance is needed. It may be necessary for the teacher to step in and give the information again or maybe to ask a few questions to guide the children's thinking. The teacher's visits also convey to the children that the adults are interested in their endeavors and view their activities as being important.

The teacher becomes aware of the child who follows directions, the one who has difficulty in assuming the responsibility of a specific task, the one who waits for an adult or another child to help him, the one who needs more challenging activities, and the one who is imaginative.

The reporting session at the end of the activity time allows the teacher to evaluate the students' progress in the short-term activity. As each child reports orally, the teacher appraises his ability to recall and explain what he has done.

This author found that in a reporting session following the activity, most children responded in complete sentences when they had something concrete to tell about and something to hold in their hands or something visual to describe.* Short-term activities with their completed products provide this optimal situation.

Prior to presenting an activity to the children, the teacher should do it herself so that she is aware of all the steps involved and the most efficient way to demonstrate them. In most presentations of procedures, the teacher does only enough to give the necessary directions. If too much is done, the children may copy exactly rather than use their own imagination and creativity.

Materials for activities should be available in a specific place so that children may easily get the necessary equipment and go to the designated area to carry out the project.

A daily record is kept of the children performing short-term activities. Pertinent comments related to the preparation for formal instruction should be noted on these records.

---

*Cowe, Eileen Grace. *A study of kindergarten activities for language development.* Unpublished doctoral dissertation, Teachers College, Columbia University, 1969, p. 86.

Some suggestions for short-term activities appropriate for young children are given in the following listings.

Food Pictures

Materials: Magazines containing pictures of foods, manila drawing paper, paste, and scissors.

Procedure: Cut out pictures of foods to make a holiday meal or to illustrate the food groups and paste on manila drawing paper.

Paper Towel Batik

Materials: Paper towels, crayons, and black tempera paint.

Procedure: With the crayons, make a design on the paper towel (crayons should be applied heavily on the paper towel). Paint the finished crayon design with a very thin black tempera paint. The paint is repelled by the crayons and will adhere only to the rest of the paper towel.

Stitchery

Materials: Dixie Mesh® rug backing, net or mesh vegetable and fruit bags, colored yarn, and a large needle or bodkin.

Procedure: Using a piece of colored yarn, sew a simple running stitch by passing the needle in and out of the mesh. Tell the children the needle is going for a walk, and make stitches in one direction and then turn and go another way. Different colors of yarns may be used in each piece of stitchery. This activity may take more than one day to complete.

Wallpaper Pictures

Materials: Pieces of wallpaper (decorators' sample wallpaper books may be obtained from a local store), 12 x 18 inch construction paper, and scissors.

Procedure: Designs or pictures of objects may be cut from the wallpaper. These may be arranged into a pretty picture and pasted on a piece of construction paper.

Shadow Boxes*

Materials: Top of egg carton or other soft cardboard box top; Elmer's Glue All®, small macaroni, paint, and string.

Procedure: Egg carton and macaroni may or may not be painted. If painted, allow to dry; then drops of glue are spaced over inside of box, and macaroni is positioned onto the spots of glue and allowed to dry. A hanger may be formed by pulling the string through holes punched in the top of the box.

Crayon Mosaics

Materials: Small bits and pieces of crayons. Clayola® modeling clay or another non-hardening or reusable non-toxic clay, hosiery boxes (either top or bottom) or any small shallow box, and clear plastic wrap.

Procedure: Spread the clay over the entire surface of the box. Place bits and pieces of the crayons into the clay to make a design. When design is completed, cover the box with plastic wrap to give the effect of a glass covering. If a hanger is desired, attach a commercial stick-on tab. Many children will need two days to complete this activity.

Books

Materials: Sheets of brown wrapping paper 12 x 18 inches, magazines, crayons, scissors, stapler, brad fasteners, and yarn.

Procedure: Fold each sheet of wrapping paper in half, making four pages, and use as many sheets as desired. Very rarely would a young child use more than two sheets, one for the pages of the book and one for the cover.

The child may use crayons and draw pictures on the pages. He may dictate a story to the teacher, which she hand writes on each page. This story should be kept to a maximum of two sentences per page.

Color books may be made by cutting colored pictures from magazines, a different color for each page or a complete book for one color. A shape booklet may be made in the same manner,

---

*Wylie, Joanne. *A creative guide for preschool teachers.* Racine, Wisconsin: Western Publishing Co., 1966, p. 107.

different shapes on each page or a booklet of all the same shapes. Pages and cover may be stapled together. Brad fasteners may be used to assemble the pages, or yarn may be pulled through the pages and tied.

String Paint

Materials: Pieces of heavy string or cord, paper straws, three or four colors of tempera paint in a foil pan with a diameter of about 3 inches, and newsprint or the classified section of the newspaper cut to a size of 12 x 18 inches.

Procedure: A "brush" prepared by the teacher is made from a 4 inch piece of straw with a 2 inch piece of string tied securely at one end. This is dipped into the paint and applied to the paper. The string trails on the paper, leaving a design of paint behind it. There should be a brush for each color of paint used.

Sponge Paint

Materials: Almost any kind of paper, preferably manila drawing paper, three or four colors of tempera paint mixed to the consistency of heavy cream and placed in separate foil pans about 3 inches in diameter, housecleaning sponge cut into pieces of about 2 x 4 inches (two or three sponges for each pan of paint).

Procedure: Dip sponge into the paint and then make a print on the paper.

Roll-on Paint

Materials: Empty bottles of Ban® Roll-On Anti-Perspirant Deodorant, liquid starch and four or five colors of tempera paint, and newsprint or the classified section of the newspaper cut to a size of 12 x 18 inches.

Procedure: The teacher fills the bottles with liquid starch and enough paint to make it a pretty color. The child uses the bottle as he would a pencil and makes designs on the newsprint. Children delight in using this as interesting pictures and designs appear.

Basket

Materials: Colored 12 x 18 or 9 x 12 inch construction paper, crepe paper or tissue paper, paste, and scissors.

Procedure: With the scissors punch a number of holes in either a 9 x 12 or 12 x 18 inch piece of construction paper. Fill holes with small pieces of colored crepe paper or colored tissue to look like flowers. Put paste on one end and roll into a cylinder. Paste and press the ends together. Paste a strip of construction paper across one end to form a handle. Orange construction paper may be used, and instead of punching holes in it, use a black or red crayon to make eyes, nose, and mouth, and you have a jack-o-lantern basket for Halloween.

Soap Painting

Materials: Dark blue or black construction paper, soap flakes, water, rotary egg beater, and mixing bowl.

Procedure: Put soap flakes into mixing bowl and add water gradually while beating with rotary egg beater. Consistency of the soap flakes should be about the same as stiffly beaten egg whites. Food coloring may be added for variety. The soap flake mixture is used as finger paints to make a picture or a design on construction paper.

Scribble Design

Materials: 9 x 12 inch manila drawing paper, 12 x 18 inch black construction paper, and assorted colors of crayons.

Procedure: Make a large scribble with a black crayon. Color in the shapes with different colored crayons. The design may be cut out and mounted on black construction paper.

Paper Tearing

Materials: A variety of shapes and sizes of colored poster paper, which is thinner than construction paper and easily torn (poster paper, not to be confused with poster board or oak tag); newsprint or newspaper may be used. Also, 9 x 12 and 12 x 18 inch pieces of colored construction paper and paste.

Procedure: Tear the poster paper or newsprint into shapes or objects. Encourage the children to tear close to the edges of the paper. This makes it easier for them to form their shapes. Formed objects may be pasted on a 9 x 12 or 12 x 18 inch piece of colored construction paper or pinned to a bulletin board. An ideal way to introduce this activity is to read the story *It Looks Like Spilt Milk*.* After reading the story, demonstrate the technique of tearing some of the shapes shown in the books. Next day, provide paper tearing as the new short-term activity.

Bakers' Clay Ornaments[†]

Materials: 1/3 cup water, 1/2 cup salt, 1 cup flour, a bowl, a baking sheet, tin foil, a sharpened pencil, poster paint, paint brushes, shellac, and yarn.

Procedure: Mix salt, water, and flour in a bowl with hands to form the clay. Take bits of the clay and make different shapes. Make a hole at the top at each shape with the point of a pencil. Place each shape on a baking sheet. Place in oven and bake for one hour at 275° F (135° C). Let shapes cool and then paint them. When the paint is dry, coat the shapes with shellac. String with yarn and use for decorations.

Nature Mosaics[‡]

Materials: Cover of a cottage cheese or margarine container, clay, glue, seeds, stones, colored pebbles, beads, shells, macaroni, or other small nature objects.

Procedure: Spread the clay over the inside surface of the container. On the clay arrange stones, pebbles, shells, seeds, etcetera, to form a design. Press the nature materials down a little in the clay.

Crinkle Painting[§]

Materials: Paper bag, three or four colors of tempera paint in foil pans with a diameter of about three inches, a pan of water, and paint brushes.

*Shaw, Charles G. *It looks like spilt milk.* New York: Harper & Row Co., 1947.

†Weiss, Ellen. *Things to make and do for Christmas.* New York: Franklin Watts, 1980, pp. 30 & 31. This is one of many excellent activities that may be found in this book. The activities may be adapted for use at any time, not just Christmas.

‡Chernoff, Goldie Taub, and Hartelius, Margaret. *Pebbles and pods: A book of nature crafts.* New York: Walker and Company, 1973.

§Seidelman, James, Mintonye, Grace, and Sherry, Kaye. *Shopping cart art.* New York: Macmillan Company, 1970, p. 6. This book has many ideas that can be adapted for short-term activities.

Procedure: Open bag out flat and wet it thoroughly on both sides. Drop different color paints all over one side of the paper. While it is still wet, crumple it as if you meant to throw it away. Open it out, press it with hands, and let it dry. Mount on colored paper.

Additional Reading

There are many books filled with ideas for short-term activities. Some examples with annotations are listed.

The REINHOLD book of arts & craft techniques for parents, teachers and children. New York: Van Nostrand Reinhold Co., 1976, 190 pp.

> This book has innumerable ideas for short-term activities. Letting children work on their own with little or no adult assistance is stressed. It also gives information on how to present techniques and materials to children according to their age level and skill.

Seidelman, James E. & Mintonye, Grace. *Creating with paper.* New York: The Macmillan Co., 1967, 57 pp.

> This book provides step-by-step directions for folding, weaving, curling, pleating, scoring, and molding paper.

Platts, Mary E. *Create a handbook for teachers of elementary art.* Benton Harbor, Michigan: Educational Service, Inc., 1966, 228 pp.

> All of the ideas and techniques are clearly given, as well as diagrams for each one. Some of the activities are too difficult for young children, but many may be adapted or simplified for use with them. It has a plethora of ideas.

Wylie, Joanne. *A creative guide for preschool teachers.* Racine, Wisconsin: Western Publishing Company, 1966, 175 pp.

> The title is certainly appropriate, as the book does cover all areas of the preschool curriculum. Teachers who are looking for ideas and suggestions for short-term activities will find this book to be of great value.

Hoover, F. Louis. *Art activities for the very young.* Worcester, Massachusetts: Davis Publications Inc., 1961, 77 pp.

> Detailed instructions are given in this book for a number of art activities, including the displaying of the children's art. In addition, explanations are given in laymen's terms of the value of children's art activities.

Seefeldt, Carol. *Social studies for the preschool-primary child.* Columbus, Ohio: Charles E. Merrill Publishing Company, 1977, 335 pp.

> The numerous ideas for activities and experiences for social studies make this a very practical and useful book. However, this is only one aspect dealt with. In describing activities, the author helps the teacher understand how to introduce concepts from the various social sciences to young children. Ideas for teaching history, geography, economics, international education, and other social sciences are presented. The text assumes that children will be taught in an educational environment where play, activity, and doing are the basis for all learning.

Stangl, Jean. *Finger painting is fun.* 1658 Calle La Cumbre, Camarillo, California 93010.

> This is an excellent book. It is the result of the author's experiences of many years of working with young children. The book opens with a brief history of finger painting. The value of finger painting is discussed, as is the materials needed to do it. Recipes are given as well as special effects and extended use of finger painting. Many of the ideas suggested in this book lend themselves to short-term activities.

Chapter 12

WOODWORKING

WOODWORKING has long been recognized as a valuable activity for young children. In 1923, *The Conduct Curriculum** gave it an important place by listing the materials, equipment, typical activities, as well as the desirable changes in thought, feeling, and conduct. Despite its general acceptance as a worthwhile activity for young children, only a few writers have dealt with woodworking with any degree of thoroughness. Many teachers do not feel secure in supervising woodworking activities, and little if any attention is given to it in college courses. However, teachers who do provide experiences with wood for their children are enthusiastic about its benefits.

Woodworking is not only a very exciting and satisfying activity in itself for many children, but it also contributes greatly to the child's general development. Few if any children have had any experiences with woodworking before entering school. Consequently, to most children it is something new and exciting to undertake. In addition to learning how to handle the tools, they learn eye-hand coordination and how to use their bodies when they work.

George Fuller says that as children progress from simple to complex in the things that they make, they learn in various ways how the parts of a thing contribute to the whole.† They learn how

---

*Burke, Agnes et al. *A conduct curriculum for the kindergarten and first grade.* New York: Charles Scribner's Sons, 1923, p. 33.

†Fuller, George. *Woodworking with children.* New York: Bank Street College of Education, 1974, pp. 8, 9.

something is not complete unless it contains this or that part; how if a certain part is missing, the whole structure will be weak; how the presence of a certain part is essential, while the presence of others may be almost a matter of taste. Children also learn about sequence, that in the process of making something, certain things must be done first, second, etc. He goes on to say that in woodworking, children learn that things just do not happen by "magic." Other things have made them happen, or someone makes them happen. If you do not do certain things, certain other things will not happen. Children learn, for example, that when parts do not fit as they should, it is probably because the parts have not been cut correctly. Or when wood splits, it may be because the nail that was used was too large in diameter, or too close to the edge.

Fuller also states that woodworking creates many problems involving size, distance, and shape relationships. A child learns that the length of nails is important. If they are too short, they will not hold; if they are too long, they will come out the other side. A child learns such spatial ideas as up, down, side, straight, crooked, curved, square, inside, outside, opposite side. The child learns that when he looks at an object there is a side (or sides) that he does not see, but which is there nevertheless. He learns that if he moves his head or body to another vantage point, or if he moves the object, he would then see the other sides. Learning these things helps to build and expand a child's spatial awareness, which feeds into his awareness of his own physical self.

The building of objects involves experiencing the effects of gravity. Children will learn how to make the base of a thing broad enough so it will stand firmly. They also learn about supports and braces to give their woodworking endeavors strength where it is needed.

Children learn to solve problems and to sustain interest in their project when it cannot be completed in one day's work.

Woodworking affords the children the opportunity to share the workspace and the tools. Children increase their vocabularies as they learn the names of the tools they are using and the names of the actions and movements they use with them.

Woodworking requires a simple, sturdy workbench with an easily adjustable vise. This may be purchased from any commercial company selling equipment for preschool and kindergarten. The Tote-L-Shop* is an innovation in elementary industrial arts, a completely self-contained work and tool center, which is easily moved. It has the exclusive feature of side panels that become work station tables for children.

Cohen and Rudolph suggest the basic tools are four to six hammers of different weights and kinds: three flat-head, 10 or 13 ounce hammers, which are most secure for beginners, some hammers with claws for pulling out or redirecting nails, and a full-size heavy, adult hammer.[†] One number 8, 12 inch, sharp, crosscut saw for straight cutting is necessary, although some tall children can use 14 or even 16 inch ones. There can be two saws if there is provision for two children to saw at the same time. A rasp is a good, safe tool for children to handle and use for smoothing a rough or splintered edge against the grain and for such shaping of the wood as rounding a corner. Later in the year, when the children are more experienced and responsible with tools, a 10 inch smoothing plane and a hand drill may be added to the supply of tools.

A 1 foot rule, a folding ruler, a yardstick, and either a fat regular pencil or a flat carpenter pencil will be necessary for measuring and marking wood. In addition, pliers are handy to have and to know about, as are large scissors for cutting string, wire, or sandpaper. A brace and bit, which does the work of the drill in a more complex fashion, should be introduced late in the year.

Screwdrivers are found among woodworking tools. However they are really not as safe as is assumed. It is unwise to have this tool available to children, especially at the beginning.

A supply of different size nails is necessary. There must be the broad-headed ones, 1 to 1 1/2 inches long, for crude and easy hammering; steel nails with sharp points that go in easily and do not split wood, ranging from 1 to 2 inches; nails of different lengths and thicknesses to fit the wood and the purpose – in

---

*Brodhead-Garrett, 4560 East 71st Street, Cleveland, Ohio 44105

†Cohen, Dorothy & Rudolph, Marguerita. *Kindergarten and early schooling.* Englewood Cliffs, New Jersey: Prentice-Hall, Inc., 1977, p. 172.

short, enough variety of nails for the child to exercise selection, discrimination, and judgment. Sandpaper of different grades of roughness should also be available.

As the children become more sophisticated and imaginative with woodworking endeavors, such items as paper clips, thumb tacks, string, rubber bands, wooden spools, and scraps of leather and cloth may be made available. Glue, shellac, thinner, tempera paint, paste wax, paper towels, paste brushes, and foil pans should be added to the list of supplies or accessories in the woodworking area.

Pine is the wood most suitable for woodworking for young children because it is the cheapest and the easiest to use. Pine is particularly soft and smooth to work with both for hammering and sawing. Balsa, poplar, and basswood are also good soft woods but are not as suitable for sawing and hammering. Often lumberyards will give away scraps. However, it is important not to take pieces of such hard wood as oak, maple, or birch, which are very difficult for children to penetrate with nails or saw, although interesting small pieces may be used for gluing in connection with woodworking.

Woodworking should be introduced several weeks after the school year commences. By this time the teacher and children have achieved a good rapport and an understanding of each other, and the general routines of the Free Play or Choice Period are well understood by all the children.

Very young and inexperienced children start woodworking by just gluing. After a few weeks, demonstrate the use of a hammer and permit two or three children to hammer. Some children will be content just to hammer nails into the wood, while others will nail pieces of wood together. Only after the children have learned the techniques of hammering may the saw be introduced; after that, the other tools may be made available. In each case, beginning with the hammer, the teacher introduces the tool to all the children, and then two, three, or maybe four children participate in woodworking.

In the beginning, the children will be satisfied to have their wood creations in the natural wood. But as time goes by, some children may want to paint them. If so, provide them with a mixture of shellac, shellac thinner, and tempera paint (powdered or liquid) in a shallow foil pan, and a paintbrush (the kind you would use for paste). The shellac thinner makes it easy to use, as it dries immediately when applied to the object. The coat of so-called paint adds dignity and a finish to the children's work. Another method of finishing a piece of woodwork is to apply paste wax with a piece of cloth or paper towel. This is most appropriate for the very young or inexperienced child.

Tools must have a specific storage space and be readily accessible to the children. Tools may be hung, by means of pegs or other devices, on a wall, a panel, or other vertical surface. The surface on which the tools are hung may be in the open or in a shallow closet with doors that are opened when they are being used. George Fuller suggests a cart that may be wheeled away and locked up when not in use.* He also says that each tool should have its assigned place. Outlines of tools may be drawn or painted on the tool panel to help the child in putting the tools away. Some workbenches are enclosed like a cabinet with ample storage place for tools. Community Playthings† has a Tool Cabinet with locking hasp and carrying handle, which is 24 inches high by 40 inches wide when opened. Tool-hanging hooks are included. Childcraft Education Corporation‡ has a Tool Organizer that is to be hung on the wall. It is a smooth-edged metal rack with cutouts to match shapes of various tool handles.

If tools are to be hung on the walls, they should be low enough so that the children can reach them easily when taking and returning them to and from their respective places.

A drawer or two and some shelves near the bench are important to hold sandpaper, other materials, and perhaps the nails. Regardless of where the nails are stored, there should be a plastic jar or tin can for each particular kind of nail. Often nails get spilled, and a fascinating way of picking up nails from the floor is, of course, with a magnet, which should also be kept in a prescribed place and put back after use.

---

*Fuller, George. *Woodworking with children*. New York: Bank Street College of Education, 1974, p. 6.

†Community Playthings, Rifton, New York 12471

‡Childcraft Education, Corp., 20 Kilmer Road, Edison, New Jersey 08817

Even with an interesting and effective introduction to woodworking, the children must be closely supervised. This being so, woodworking may not be offered every day. The teacher's close supervision is to make sure the children use the tools correctly and obey the safety rules. After several sessions, the teacher may find that it is not necessary to give them close attention and that merely keeping an eye on them provides sufficient supervision.

Sometimes the teacher may quietly observe the children while they work, or she may be a contributor by asking questions or pointing out interesting features of their projects. The teacher may need to help a child in making an object broad enough so it will stand firmly. She also may need to give some children encouragement to continue with their projects.

Four publications that give valuable information on conducting woodworking with young children are listed. *Woodworking With Children*,* a booklet written by an experienced woodworking teacher, covers all aspects of the activity in a comprehensive manner. Dorothy Cohen and Marguerita Rudolph[†] give an excellent listing of materials and accessories.

Woodworking For Children[‡] is an excellent pamphlet written by Mary W. Moffitt, an authority in this area, and speaks to the inexperienced and the experienced teacher.

The Little Carpenter[§] contains pictures of all the tools that are used in woodworking, a valuable resource to the teacher in ordering tools and learning more about them.

The teacher should be evaluating the progress of the children as they participate in woodworking activities. She will be able to observe if they are using the tools properly, if eye-hand coordination is improving, and if the woodworking endeavors are more complex.

The teacher will also be able to evaluate students' progress as

---

*Fuller, George. *Woodworking with children.* New York: Bank Street College of Education, 1974, 22 pp.

†Cohen, Dorothy & Rudolph, Marguerita. *Kindergarten & early schooling.* Englewood Cliffs, New Jersey: Prentice-Hall, Inc. 1977, pp. 168-179.

‡Moffitt, Mary W. *Woodworking for children*, New York: Early Childhood Education Council of New York, 1976.

§ *The little carpenter.* New Britain, Connecticut: Stanley Tools 06050 they tell about their experiences during the daily reporting session. As each child reports orally, the teacher will observe the child's ability to recall, explain, and answer questions about his project.

Chapter 13

COOKING

PREPARING food and eating it has been enjoyed by all ethnic groups from the beginning of time. So it is little wonder that cooking and eating have a place in the preschool and kindergarten curriculum. Making butter, cooking applesauce, and popping corn were some of the cooking experiences carried on at the Horace Mann Kindergarten in the early 1920s.

Cooking experiences give children firsthand opportunities to observe, experiment, explore, wonder, and discover as they manipulate dough, see liquids change into solids, observe what happens when one ingredient is added to another, and see the effect of heat and cold upon certain products.

Young children are in the sensorimotor stage of development, so that manipulating dough, stirring cakes and puddings, seeing, smelling, touching, hearing, and tasting are excellent ways of learning.

Science learnings occur as they observe ice cream freeze or melt and yeast breads rise. Mathematical concepts are formed as children measure and see 1/2 cup, 1 teaspoon, and 1 tablespoon of ingredients.

Reading activities are taking place as they hear or read and follow the directions of a recipe. Vocabularies are increased during cooking activities when such words as scrape, beat, whip, refrigerate, brown, squeeze, chop, press, and melt are used. The utensils used for cooking acquaint children with new words and new concepts. Mixing bowl, egg beater, paring knife, measuring cup, grater, serrated-edge knife, and spatula take on new meaning when children use them. When the texture of food is discussed, words such as stiff, stringy, lumpy, creamy, crunchy, firm, and crisp soon become part of the children's vocabularies. This is also true when the flavor of food is described using tart, salty, sweet, tangy, bitter, and sour.

Health and safety principles are employed when children take care to wash hands, to be careful around hot plates or stoves, and to take time to wipe up spills. Children can learn the names of the foods they are preparing and eating.

*Cool Cooking for Kids** suggest the following basic and optional equipment.

Basic Equipment

Rotary egg beater
Hot plate with 1 or 2 burners
Electric skillet
Paring knife (sharp)
4 stainless steel or plastic mixing bowls of graduated sizes
Flour sifter
Biscuit and cookie cutters in many shapes
Pot Holders
Large, two-tined fork
2 wooden mixing spoons
2 cookie sheets
Pyrex saucepan with lid (1½ quarts)
Rolling pin

Spatulas, short- and long-bladed
Pancake turners, short- and long-handled
An apron for each child, and a chef's hat if possible
Clock timer
Measuring spoons
Measuring cups (fractional for dry ingredients and Pyrex for liquids)
2 muffin tins (12 wells each)
Wooden cutting board
Rubber scraper
Clean-up equipment, (dishpan, soap, washcloths, towels, drainer, sponge)
Cooling rack

Optional Equipment

Electric griddle
Corn popper
Pyrex custard cups (1 for each child)
Strainer

Tray, for holding food and equipment
Portable refrigerator
Blender

*McClenahan, Pat & Jaqua, Ida. *Cool cooking for kids.* Belmont, California: Fearon Publishers, 1976, p. 12.

It is best to buy sturdy, well-made equipment. This equipment should be used only for actual cooking experiences and should be stored in a special place away from the kitchen tools that are used for dramatic play.

Cooking is a short-term activity and may be done once a week, once a month, at holiday time, or whenever the teacher wishes to do it. All of the children may be involved, or a group of five or six children may prepare the food to be enjoyed by all.

One way of managing the whole class and giving everyone an opportunity to be involved in the project is to arrange the children in a semicircle, or around the mixing activity. Everyone should be able to watch what goes on, and children may take turns in measuring and stirring. The children should be seated either in chairs or on the floor; this requires that the mixing activity take place low enough so the children can see easily. If low enough table is not available, cover an area with clean paper and use the floor. A recipe that works well with this arrangement is —

JIFFY FUDGE

1 3 ounce pkg. soft cream cheese
1 lb. confectioner's sugar
3 tablespoons water
1 teaspoon vanilla
3 1 oz. packets melted unsweetened chocolate
1 cup broken walnuts

How to Prepare:

1. Stir cream cheese until smooth.
2. Add water and vanilla to cheese; stir.
3. Add sugar to cheese mixture; beat smooth.
4. Quickly add the chocolate; stir.
5. Then add the walnuts.
6. Spread this mixture into a well-buttered pan; chill 1 hr.

A cookie or gingerbread men recipe may be used with the whole class. However, there is another step.

When the mixing is finished, the children may work in groups of five or six to cut out gingerbread men, cookies, or to roll the dough into balls and to decorate them. This continues until each child has had an opportunity. A recipe to use with this procedure is —

EASY DOO-ZITS

2 1/2 cups graham cracker crumbs (about 1 1/2 pkgs.)
1/2 cup sugar
1 tsp. cinnamon
1 tsp. nutmeg

Mix all together and add:

1 cup peanut butter
2/3 cup light Karo syrup

How to Prepare:

1. Mix and roll into balls.
2. Roll in powdered sugar and chill.
(Makes 45. If you prefer the cookies not to be so sweet, use less sugar and Karo syrup.)

Vegetable soup may be made with five or six children preparing part of the vegetables, then five or six more preparing some and continuing until all have had a turn.

VEGETABLE SOUP

Vegetables
Bay leaf
Thyme
Beef bouillon cube

How to Prepare:

Wash, peel, or scrape vegetables. Cut into pieces. Place in kettle, and put enough water in to cover vegetables. Add a bay leaf, a pinch of thyme, and a beef bouillon cube. Cook until vegetables are tender. Then add salt and pepper to taste.

Harvest Salad may be made by having five or six children work at one time, each preparing his own recipe. A recipe to use is —

HARVEST SALAD

Apples
Carrots
Grapes

Raisins
Yogurt

How to Prepare:

Wash and cut apples in sections. Each child may cut a section on a wax paper square with a case knife, cutting downward, and empty into his small paper or plastic dish or paper cup. Wash and cut carrots. (Scrape if necessary.) Each child may mix one spoonful with cut apples. Grapes may be washed and add to salad mixture. Add small spoonful of raisins and 1 teaspoon yogurt.

Five or six children may participate in corn popping, gathering around and watching through the glass top as the kernels burst into white fluffs, and then another group may take their turn with another popperful of corn. This continues until all have had the experience.

When using this procedure, children who are not engaged in the cooking activity should be involved in one of the basic activities, such as housekeeping, library, or table toys. If there is only one adult in the room, it will be necessary to limit the choices to activities that can be carried on without the teacher making her frequent visits.

Cooking experiences always demand the constant supervision of an adult, but cooking should not be simply a demonstration. The children should be involved as much as possible. Direct involvement will help sustain interest and attention. In preparing some recipes, children can taste and smell each ingredient separately before it is added and again after it is mixed. The teacher should encourage children to talk about what they and others are doing. This helps keep attention and enables children to understand the process. The children will also enjoy a descriptive chant about the actions, such as "This is the way we chop the nuts." When children have had a cooking experience at school, copies of the recipes may be sent home.

The following are some excellent publications that give helpful suggestions and recipes:

Austin AEYC. *Ideas for planning.* Washington, D.C.: NAEYC, 1973, 52 pp.

Brody, Judy Lederman. *Shake, batter and roll.* Williamsville, New York: Apple-A-Day Publications, 1978, 69 pp.

Croft, Doreen. *Recipes for busy little hands.* 741 Maplewood Place, Palo Alto, California 94303, 1967, 46 pp.

Johnson, Barbara & Plemons, Betty. *Cup cooking.* P.O. Box 1177, Lake Alfred, Florida 33850: Early Educators Press, 1981, 48 pp.

May, Billie. *Creating with materials* (leaflet 10). Washington, D.C.: Association for Childhood Education International, 1969, 4 pp.

McAfee, Oralie, Haines, Evelyn W., Young, Barbara Bullman, Markun, & Maloney, Patricia. *Cooking and eating with children.* Washington, D.C.: Association for Childhood Education International, 1974, 48 pp.

McClenahan, Pat & Jaqua, Ida. *Cool cooking for kids.* Belmont, California: Fearon Publishers, Inc., 1976, 176 pp.

Puckett, Margaret & Wright, Pat. *Macaroni, spaghetti, and oodles of noodles.* Fort Worth, Texas: Branch-Smith, Inc., 66 pp.

Stangl, Jean. *The no-cook cookery cookbook.* 1658 Calle La Cumbre, Camarillo, California 93010, 49 pp.

Tannenbaum, Lona (Ed.). *The New York cooking experience.* Early Childhood Education Council of New York, 66 Leroy Street, New York, New York 10014.

Wanamaker, Nancy, Hearn, Kristin, Richarz, Sherrill, & Idaho-Washington AEYC. *More than graham crackers.* Washington, D.C.: NAEYC, 1979, 93 pp.

The National Dairy Council gives workshops for teachers and publishes material about nutrition. The main office is located at 111 N. Canal Street, Chicago, Illinois 60606, and there are several regional offices.

Chapter 14

ROOM ARRANGEMENT

LIFE in a classroom is experienced as satisfying, interesting, meaningful, and conducive to growth when the equipment and supplies are arranged to invite children to become involved. Much of the equipment and materials are used over an extended period. Others are added as they seem advisable to the situation and timing.

In addition to the centers of interest that are the focus of this book, there are other areas in the classroom that are regularly used for a particular purpose. Such areas are those for eating, resting, and assembling the total group for sharing, discussion, music, or story.

The size and appearance of these areas and the centers of interest will vary depending on the equipment and the overall size and shape of the individual classroom. There is no single ideal classroom arrangement. However, effective functioning within the room requires the equipment and materials to be organized with certain factors in mind.

The first factor for the teacher to consider is to make sure that each area or center is clearly defined. This will help to provide an organized, structured environment for the children. A mistake often made in room arrangement is placing the furniture along the walls and leaving an open space in the middle of the room, thus creating an open area that invites the children to run and chase each other. To avoid this, place something in a roughly central position to break up the space; for example, a bookcase, shelves, or a screen which may be used to define a specific area.

Where centers cannot be set off with portable bookcases or other physical barriers, rugs, may be used to provide a boundary line for a given center. This will give the centers some physical definition and will encourage the children to stay on the rug when using the area. In the preceding chapters, suggestions for ways to define and set off areas have also been made. The film *Organizing Free Play** gives helpful and useful suggestions and techniques to use when setting up a room.

Two excellent books that deal with creating a functional and pleasant environment for young children are *Arranging the Informal Classroom*† and *Room To Learn.*‡

The second factor to keep in mind is classroom traffic. It should be minimized, and the necessary traffic should flow freely. Equipment items and storage facilities should be located as close as possible to the classroom area in which they are ordinarily used, thus minimizing the distances that children must move the equipment and materials when they take them out or return them. To keep traffic flowing freely, avoid cross traffic. For example, children should be able to enter or leave the housekeeping area or library without walking through children's block constructions. Traffic routes leading to the doorway, toilet facilities, drinking fountain, or other heavily used lanes should be free from obstructions.

The third factor to be considered is noise. The block and woodworking area should be kept away from centers that involve activities demanding close concentration by the children. Adherence to this factor will help maximize each child's independence and minimize the frequency with which the teacher must stop to warn noisy children to quiet down. Needless to say, sound-absorbent walls and ceilings are very helpful in controlling the noise level in a classroom.

Storage is the fourth factor. The arrangement of storage facilities and cleanup equipment should be such that it encourages

---

*Film *Organizing free play*. B/W, 22 min. MTP9053 Modern Talking Picture Service, Inc., or Headstart, 1200 19th Street, N.W., Washington, D.C. 20505.

†Engel, Brenda S. *Arranging the informal classroom*. Newton, Massachusetts: Education Development Center, Inc., 1973, 88 pp.

‡Dean, Joan. *Room to learn*. New York: Citation Press, 1974, 137 pp.

the children to be independent in using and putting things away. Arts and crafts or so-called messy activities should be located near the sink if there is one in the classroom, and any activity involving significant cleanup should include appropriate cleanup materials as well as the equipment for the activity itself. There should be easy access to cubbyholes and other storage facilities that are used frequently by the children.

Lighting is the fifth factor to consider when arranging an environment for young children. Ideally, all areas of the classroom should be adequately lighted. If this is not the case, be sure to locate areas requiring careful visual inspection or discrimination near windows or lights, placing areas not requiring fine visual discrimination in the darker areas of the room.

As the teacher makes frequent visits to the various areas during the Free Play or Choice Period, she should be checking to see if the equipment and supplies are arranged in the best possible way.

INDEX

TEXAS A&M UNIVERSITY-TEXARKANA